Chinyere Felicia Priest's *The Conversion of Igbo Christians to Islam: A Study of Religious Change in a Christian Heartland* is a must-read for scholars and students of religion in Africa and all those interested in patterns of religious change. Building on ethnographic field research in Igboland, Nigeria's dominant Christian homeland, the author succinctly explores the reasons behind the conversion of Igbo Christians to Islam. In doing this, she leaves no one in doubt of the diverse results for religious realignments in any environment and among different people groups.

Egodi Uchendu, PhD
Professor of History,
University of Nigeria, Nsukka, Nigeria
Author, *Dawn for Islam in Eastern Nigeria*

Few researchers have undertaken an empirical study of the phenomena behind the mass conversion of Igbo people to Islam like this author. In my view, the findings of this research are very stunning. This book is a wake-up call to the church to re-examine its method of teachings and the discipleship of its converts. It convincingly highlights when and how Islam, an alien religion, began its gradual but steady incursion into Igboland, an erstwhile bastion of Christianity, and the rationale for its amazing success. The church in Igboland must be intentional in checking this Islamic penetration, without which the base of Christianity in Eastern Nigeria would be seriously eroded in no distant time. This book is a must-read for all scholars, church leaders, and Bible school and theological students.

Pastor Austen C. Ukachi
Senior Pastor, He's Alive Chapel, Lagos, Nigeria
Member, National Advisory Council,
Pentecostal Fellowship of Nigeria

Nigeria is a land believed to be a locale where noxious rivalries among the Nigerian ethnic peoples exist and are acerbated by geopolitical and religious divides to the extent that Muslims control the North and Christians hold sway in the South. The South-East geopolitical zone is occupied predominantly by Igbo people with their religious bent to Christianity. It is due to this inner capacity for experiencing God in Christ, that Igboland is described by some religious studies scholars as "the heart of Christianity." There had been a growing consensus among religious scholars in the past that Islam never appealed to the Igbo, especially when every effort to introduce Islam into Igboland was greeted with constant rebuff.

But it is a fact that some Igbo people are now being converted to Islam. This is why the study carried out by Chinyere Priest, *The Conversion of Igbo Christians to Islam*, is germane at this critical point in time. Chinyere's work will help to distil what is true from what is false. I sincerely commend this book to all and sundry, particularly to serious-minded and heavenly conscious individuals in whom I know that this work will produce such a magnetic effect that will propel them into loving evangelism in Igboland.

Rev Mbachi Valentine Chukwujekwu, PhD
Department of Religion and Human Relations,
Nnamdi Azikiwe University, Awka, Nigeria

The Conversion of Igbo Christians to Islam

A Study of Religious Change in a Christian Heartland

Chinyere Felicia Priest

MONOGRAPHS

© 2020 Chinyere Felicia Priest

Published 2020 by Langham Global Library
An imprint of Langham Publishing
www.langhampublishing.org

Langham Publishing and its imprints are a ministry of Langham Partnership

Langham Partnership
PO Box 296, Carlisle, Cumbria, CA3 9WZ, UK
www.langham.org

ISBNs:
978-1-78368-779-4 Print
978-1-83973-011-5 ePub
978-1-83973-012-2 Mobi
978-1-83973-013-9 PDF

Chinyere Felicia Priest has asserted her right under the Copyright, Designs and Patents Act, 1988 to be identified as the Author of this work.

All rights reserved. No part of this publication may be reproduced, stored in a retrieval system or transmitted, in any form or by any means, electronic, mechanical, photocopying, recording or otherwise, without the prior written permission of the publisher or the Copyright Licensing Agency.

Requests to reuse content from Langham Publishing are processed through PLSclear. Please visit www.plsclear.com to complete your request.

Scriptures taken from the Holy Bible, New International Version®, NIV®. Copyright © 1973, 1978, 1984, 2011 by Biblica, Inc.™ Used by permission of Zondervan.

British Library Cataloguing-in-Publication Data
A catalogue record for this book is available from the British Library

ISBN: 978-1-78368-779-4

Cover & Book Design: projectluz.com

Langham Partnership actively supports theological dialogue and an author's right to publish but does not necessarily endorse the views and opinions set forth here or in works referenced within this publication, nor can we guarantee technical and grammatical correctness. Langham Partnership does not accept any responsibility or liability to persons or property as a consequence of the reading, use or interpretation of its published content.

I dedicate this work:

to God, who spared my life and gave me a second
chance to live and complete this dissertation;

to my dearly beloved husband,
Victor Priest Chukwuma,
who supports me in all situations;

to all the Igbo converts to Islam who supplied
the data used for this work.

Contents

Acknowledgements xiii
Abstract xv
Chapter 1 1
  Introduction
    Background and Motivation for This Study 1
    Research Problem 2
    Purpose of the Research 3
    Objectives of Study 3
    Research Questions 3
      Main Research Question 3
      Sub-Research Questions 4
    Assumptions of the Study 4
    Significance of the Research 4
    Limitations 5
    Delimitations 6
    Operational Definition 7
    Conceptual Framework 7

Chapter 2 11
  Literature Review
    Introduction 11
    A Brief History of Igbo 11
      Culture 12
      Government 16
      Igbo Traditional Religion 17
      Igbo Cosmology 22
    Christianity in Igboland 27
      The Missionaries' Techniques 30
      Igbo Response to Christianity 33
    The Igbo and Islam 38
    Conversion 43
      Conversion: Interdisciplinary Perspectives 47
      Anthropology 47
      Historians 55
      Sociology 59
      Psychology 67

  Christian Understanding of Conversion...69
  Denominational Perspectives of Conversion 74
   Evangelicals 74
   Pentecostals...75
   Mainline Protestants...76
   Catholics 77
   Orthodox...79
  Islamic Understanding of Conversion 81
  Biblical Understanding of Conversion...85
   Old Testament Conversion 86
   New Testament Conversion 88
  Factors Influencing Religious Conversion 94
  Conclusion 96

Chapter 3 99
Research Methodology
  Research Design..99
  The Rationale for Qualitative Research 99
  Setting and Participants 101
  Sample Procedures 102
  Data Collection Procedures...103
   Interview 103
   Observations...104
   Digital Recording 105
  Data Analysis 105
   Organizing the Data 105
   Immersion in the Data..106
   Coding the Data 106
   Interpreting the Findings 106
   Validating the Findings..107
   Reporting Findings 107
  Site Entry...107
  Ethical Consideration 108

Chapter 4 109
Findings and Interpretation
  Introduction 109
  Findings...109
   Sub-Research Question 1: What Are the Backgrounds
   (Social, Religious, and Familial) of the Converts? 109

Sub-Research Question 2: What Are the Stages
    of Their Conversion?..119
Main Research Question: What Are the Igbo Converts'
    Reasons for Their Conversion to Islam?...................128
Sub-research Question 4: How Have They Changed as a
    Result of Their Conversion? 141
Other Emerging Themes..148
    Igbo Christians' Response to Igbo Muslims' Theological
        Objections 148
    Igbo Muslims' Position on Jihad 149
    Igbo Converts' Justification of Their Conversion.......150
    Existing Relationship between Muslim-Christian Spouses
        and Their Children..151

Chapter 5 155
Discussion, Conclusion and Recommendations
    Introduction 155
    Summary of the Findings..156
    Discussion 159
    An Examination of the Findings in Relation to
        Existing Research 161
    Highlights of Interesting, New or Unexpected
        Findings Discovered 166
    Contributions or Practical Applications of the Study.......168
        Scholarship 168
        The Church in Igboland 169
        Missiology 170
        To the Researcher 170
    Recommendations 170
        To the Church in Igboland 170
        To the Igbo Christian People 173
        To CAPRO Missionaries in Igboland and the Church 173
        To the Igbo Muslims in Igboland..............................174
    Limitations of the Study and Recommendations for
        Future Research...174

Bibliography.. 177

List of Tables

Table 1. Conversion motifs...9

Table 2. Summary of the descriptive elements of the converts 118

Table 3. Stages of the converts' conversion process..127

Table 4. Parallel conversion process of Gerlach and Hine and Rambo 128

List of Figures

Figure 1. Church affiliation of participants..113

Figure 2. Interaction typology between converts and families 126

Figure 3. Conversion motifs of the converts 129

Acknowledgements

I give thanks to my sweet and precious children, Urudinachi and Chimma, who went through the agonizing trauma of ill health with me during the writing period.

I am grateful to my supervisor, Dr Steven H. Rasmussen, for his diligent commitment to me, my family, and to this work. You were not only interested in my study, but in every aspect of my life bringing comfort and succor in my time of trials. *Chukwu gozie gi*! (God bless you!)

I am grateful to Professor Egodi Uchendu whose academic works provided in-depth understanding on the history and arrival of Islam in Igbo. Her warm reception dispelled my fear and anxiety the first time I met her. Thank you.

To Africa International University kids who enriched my life with "love" letters, visits, prayers and love. You guys are priceless!

Abstract

Conversion to Islam is increasingly growing in areas formerly hostile to Islam. The current study was carried out to identify the reasons responsible for the Igbo[1] Christians' conversion to Islam.

Extensive examination of related literature and previous works on religious conversion revealed that conversion is more of a gradual process rather than instantaneous.

To identify why Igbo Christians are converting to Islam, qualitative research method was employed. Data were collected via in-depth, face-to-face ethnographic interviews with thirty (twenty-three males and seven females) Igbo Christians who had converted to Islam.

The interviews revealed seven reasons. These are: (1) Intellectual (Islam is more logical and rational behaviorally; a negative lifestyle within the local church), (2) affectional (Muslims are upright, caring, and loving), (3) mystical (dreams and divine encounter), (4) experimental (giving Islam a try and embraced it in the process), (5) coercion (pressurized to convert), (6) desire for upward mobility, and (7) desire to become a Reverend or minister and still have a family. Intellectual and affectional motifs were the most motivating reasons given for conversion.

The findings indicate that there is need for intellectual engagement of the biblical doctrine in the church. In other words, the church needs to systematically and adequately explain the doctrine of the Trinity, sonship of Christ, and original sin to members. Given the significant relationship between the intellectual motif and the Igbo Christian conversion to Islam, this must no longer be given cursory attention. It is recommended that the church should

---

1. Though sometimes referred to as Ibo, this work will use Igbo throughout.

wake from her slumber and nominalism, and to begin discipling, mentoring and equipping Christians to adequately respond to Muslim objections to the gospel.

CHAPTER 1

Introduction

Background and Motivation for This Study

After having served as a missionary in various parts of Muslim West Africa and Sudan, in a bid to see Christ ardently worshipped among Muslims there, I returned home in 2012 and learned that my own people, the Igbo, were converting to Islam. This realization was heartrending and overwhelming. I wept day and night for my people, and began seeking evidence for the cause of this phenomenon. I read some online Muslim *da'wees'* conversations sharing how Christians in the Nigerian universities were converting to Islam in large numbers. This knowledge further wrenched my heart and sparked an interest to investigate the reasons why the Igbo were converting to Islam.

In recent years, conversion to Islam has significantly increased in areas formerly hostile to Islam. For instance, good numbers of Americans are converting to Islam, South Korean Christians are converting to Islam, and native-born British as well.[1] This phenomenon is also being observed in Igboland, the Christian heartland of Nigeria,[2] where a growing number of mosques, Islamic schools/institutions, and Igbo converts to Islam can be observed. Though most people have argued that the Igbo are converting to Islam primarily for the economic motif, which may have been accurate in the past, closer examination shows that this is no longer the case. According to this current research, the Igbo are nowadays primarily converting to Islam for

---

1. Köse and Loewenthal, *Conversion to Islam.*
2. Nnorom, "Islam in Igboland."

the intellectual motif. This claim is significant because it is often deemed that the Igbo are obsessed with money, thus it is assumed their conversion to Islam is in order to acquire money, but the current research would dispute this assumption.

Chapter 2 of this work discusses the relevant literature on the Igbo and religious conversion, the following chapter discusses my chosen methodology, chapter 4 reveals my interpretations of the data and my findings, and the final chapter discusses the relevance of these findings, with my conclusions and recommendations for moving forward.

Research Problem

This research is aimed at identifying contemporary Igbo converts' reasons for their conversion to Islam. The Igbo, who perceived Islam a foreign religion and a taboo to embrace it, resisting its penetration during the nineteenth-century Islamic jihad of Dan Fodio in Nigeria, are now voluntarily converting to Islam. Chukwuemeka Odumegwu Ojukwu expressed the traditional Igbo disdain of Islam thus:

> Our Biafran ancestors remained immune from the Islamic contagion. From the middle years of the last century Christianity was established in our land. In this way we came to be a predominantly Christian people. We came to stand out as a non-Muslim island in a raging Islamic sea. Throughout the period of the ill-fated Nigerian experiment, the Muslims hoped to infiltrate Biafra by peaceful means and quiet propaganda, but failed. Then the late Ahmadu Bello, the Sardauna of Sokoto tried, by political and economic blackmail and terrorism, to convert Biafrans settled in Northern Nigeria to Islam. His hope was that these Biafrans of dispersion would then carry Islam to Biafra, and by so doing give the religion political control of the area.[3]

Today, the Igbo are not converting to Islam forcefully, but voluntarily and peacefully. There are an "increased number of mosques and Islamic institutions, growing numbers of well-educated Igbo Muslim leaders, and the

---

3. Ojukwu, *Ahiara Declaration*, 68.

obvious affluence and influence of Igbo Muslim converts in Igboland."[4] C. Aham Nnorom raised the alarm that the Igbo community is in trouble due to the increased number of Igbo Muslims, Islamic institutions, and mosques in Igboland. Simon Ottenberg, an anthropologist who first observed this phenomenon, was amazed because this behavior seemed odd to Igbo nature. This phenomenon may breed hostility and violence among the Igbo people[5] as the Igbo converts no longer share the same religious faith with non-Igbo Muslims. The Igbo Muslim women would rather marry the Hausa Muslims instead of getting married to a non-Igbo Muslim man, while the men endeavor to marry Igbo Christian women in an attempt to increase their number and infiltrate Igbo communities.

Purpose of the Research

The purpose of this study is to identify the reasons former Igbo Christians give for their conversion to Islam.

Objectives of Study

1. To identify reported factors that influence Igbo Christians' conversion to Islam.
2. To identify the social, religious and family backgrounds of the Igbo converts to Islam.
3. To discover how conversion to Islam transforms/changes the lives of these Igbo Christian converts.

Research Questions

Main Research Question

The main research question that this work will explore is, what reasons do the Igbo Christians give for their conversion to Islam?

---

4. Nnorom, "Islam in Igboland," 16.
5. Nnorom, 241.

Sub-Research Questions

In order to clarify the main research question, the following sub-questions were addressed by means of qualitative, empirical research:
1. What are the backgrounds (social, religious, and family) of the converts?
2. What are the stages of their conversion?
3. Which conversion motifs are involved in their conversion?
4. How have their lives changed as a result of their conversion?

Assumptions of the Study

The research findings were evaluated based on the following assumptions. First, the Bible is the basis for defining conversion theologically from a Christian point of view. Second, the interviewees were mostly telling the truth from their perspective, although they may be trying to present themselves and their religion as well as possible.

Significance of the Research

This researcher believes the study has great importance in areas affecting the church, missiology, policymaking, the Igbo community, missionaries to the Igbo, and the preservation of Igbo Muslims in the following ways:

Significance to the Church

The research awakens the church to the quiet, but aggressive, incursion of Islam into Igboland. This should encourage the churches to foster programs of Muslim evangelism. Outreach can only happen through intensive mission awareness and mobilization of the church in Igboland to engage in Muslim evangelism.

Significance to Missiology

This research is relevant for the academic field of missiology, adding to the corpus of research data and providing an important contribution to the understanding of the conversion of Christians to Islam in general, and of the Igbo people in particular. A significant number of studies exist that deal with conversion from Islam to Christianity, but not many exist on conversion from

Christianity to Islam. Furthermore, this research adds to the work of Igbo scholars regarding Islam and the Igbo people as there are few Igbo scholarly studies on this topic to date.

Significance to Policymakers

This study will enable policymakers to craft policies with greater understanding and consideration of Islam by encouraging Christians to read the Qur'an and the tenets of the Islamic faith in order to foster a cordial co-existence between the adherents of the two faiths. The findings of this study would also encourage the government to create a feasible model regarding how Christian-Muslim relations can best exist harmoniously in Igboland, despite their different ideologies of the religions.

Significance to the Igbo Community

This study will enlighten and encourage the Igbo community in maintaining unity for the sake of posterity and the healthy survival of the Igbo nation.

Significance to Missionaries

The research provides valuable information for missionaries serving among Igbo Muslims, providing them with the reasons why Igbo Christians report they convert to Islam. This information can be used to inform training and witnessing in order to equip and mobilize outreach to these Igbo Muslim converts and those Igbo Christians considering conversion.

Significance to Igbo Muslims

This research will reveal that Islam is making inroads in Igboland (a region known as the Christian heartland of Nigeria), as Igbos are converting to the religion and spreading Islam to other Igbo communities. This knowledge would enable them to persevere in the midst of the persecution they undergo from their Christian families when they convert to Islam.

Limitations

This research was limited to a particular sample of converts, which cannot be taken as representative of all conversions to Islam, as it was limited to Igbo Christian converts to Islam and not indigenous Igbo Muslims. Because this research is focused on understanding the phenomenon of Christian conversion to Islam among the Igbo, the findings may not be transferable to other settings. However, this potential limitation was reduced by fully exploring the conversion experiences of the selected sample through in-depth, face-to-face ethnographic interviews and observations. The most suitable participants were selected from among the Igbo for the research based on the experience of their conversions from Christianity to Islam, the phenomenon under study.

The research was limited by the number of women that could be interviewed, as there were relatively few female Igbo converts to Islam that could be found in Igboland. There were a good number of indigenous Muslim Igbo women, but few who had converted from Christianity.

Furthermore, the qualitative methodology adopted poses a limitation regarding the ability to generalize and replicate findings to a different context. Time and money were also limiting factors. I had no funding for the research and the stipulated time to complete the dissertation posed a challenge, as I live and study on the other side of the continent. Due to this, I had to limit my scope of interviews to Igbo Christian converts to Islam living in Igboland. I did not extend the scope of the research area to Igbo women converts to Islam in other parts of Nigeria, where some of them now reside.

An additional potential limitation foreseen was difficulty in assessing confidential information; some people may be cautious or discreet in revealing the motives behind their conversion to Islam. However, this potential limitation seemed unfounded as many converts freely narrated their stories without hesitation. The few informants who seemed cautious were asked the questions differently to elucidate a more complete response.

Delimitations

The study was narrowed to identifying the reasons Igbo Christian converts to Islam give for their conversions. There were other related problems that could have been included, but were rejected or screened off because they were not considered consequential.

This research was limited to only Igbo Christian converts to Islam in Igboland not in other parts of Nigeria. Indigenous Igbo Muslims were not involved because Igbo-born Muslims do not experience the religious conversion from Christianity that is under study.

Operational Definition

The following terms used in this research were defined thus:

Motif: In this study, "motif" is defined as "reasons, intensions, and purposes" that a person identifies as their cause to act in a certain way.

Conversion: The term "conversion" is complex and varies in its usage and meaning. Scholars in different fields of study assign it different meanings. In this study, conversion is used as a change from one religion to another (for instance Christianity to Islam or Islam to Christianity). However, "biblical conversion" is used for how the Bible understands conversion to truly following Jesus Christ. "Islamic conversion" is how conversion to Islam is understood by Muslims. Transformation is used for conversion from a nominal to a more committed adherence to the theology of another religion or within the same religion.

Conceptual Framework

The theory adopted in this study is "conversion motif theory." It was developed by John Lofland and Norman Skonovd and was used to study the conversion motif of seventy British-born Christian converts to Islam by Ali Köse and Kate Miriam Loewenthal. A. U. Mehmedoglu and H. C. Kim adopted it in their study of South Korean converts to Islam. The theory indicates that there are six motifs that influence conversion, which they termed "conversion motifs," and are as follows:

1. Intellectual: The potential converts begin with individual and private investigation about the new religion through reading books, watching television, attending lectures, and other impersonal ways of acquainting themselves with the ideologies and way of life of the new religion.
2. Mystical: This conversion motif is dramatic, sudden and induced by voices and visions. This is what some scholars call "born again," "Damascus Road experience," "Pauline," "evangelical," etc. This experience cannot be expressed in logical and coherent terms, and is thereby termed mystical.
3. Experimental: The prospective convert takes a pragmatic "show me" attitude, ready to give the (new religious) process a try, but withholding judgment for a considerable length of time after

taking up the lifestyle of a fully committed participant, including making significant sacrifices.
4. Affectional: The thesis of this motif is that personal attachments, or strong liking for practicing believers, is central to the conversion process. In other words, "personal experience of being loved, nurtured, and affirmed by a group are central to the conversion."[6]
5. Revivalist: This motif refers to a managed or manipulated ecstatic arousal in a group, or collective context, that has a transforming effect on the individual. A good example would be the early seventies revivalist waves experienced in East Africa (Uganda).
6. Coercive: This motif "entails an extremely high degree of external pressure over a relatively long period of time, during which there is intense arousal of fear and uncertainty, culminating in empathetic identification and even love."[7] The following terms well explain the coercive conversion motif: "brainwashing," "programming," or "mind control."

Lofland and Skonovd showed variations that distinguish each of these six conversion motifs by adopting five independent variables: the degree of social pressure on the potential convert, the temporal duration of the conversion experience, the level of affective arousal, the affective content and the belief-participation sequence.[8] The following table explains these conversion motifs vividly.

The strength of this theory is its categorization of the motifs which enables researchers to classify reasons for conversion into these various categories. This model is a classic as it is also being adopted by researchers from various disciplines other than sociology. Most importantly, the authors' 1981 prediction that intellectual and experimental motifs would be on the increase has been fulfilled. Most contemporary studies on conversion utilizing this model, reveal that the experimental, and especially the intellectual motifs are on the increase, while the revivalist motif is decreasing, as they predicted. In the era of their research, the revivalist motif was on the increase.

---

6. Kim and Mehmedoglu, "Conversion Motifs," 124.
7. Lofland and Skonovd, "Conversion Motifs," 383.
8. Lofland and Skonovd, 375.

Table 1. Conversion motifs[9]

Major Variations	1. Intellectual	2. Mystical	3. Experimental	4. Affectional	5. Revivalist	6. Coercive
1. Degree of social pressure	Low or none	None or little	Low	Med.	High	High
2. Temporal duration	Med.	Short	Long	Long	Short	Long
3. Level of affective arousal	Med.	High	Low	Med.	High	High
4. Affective content	Illumination	Awe, love, fear	Curiosity	Affection	Love (and fear)	Fear (and love)
5. Belief-participation sequence	Belief-participation	Belief-participation	Participation-belief	Participation-belief	Participation-belief	Participation-belief

The theory is not encompassing, in that it is not comprehensive. There are other motifs that influence conversion that were not considered. Also, it is "narrow in the specific sense that it adduces types, but does not go on to delineate steps, phases, or processes within each type."[10] To apply the theory in this study requires that the conversion biographies of participants are evaluated or assessed according to this model, in order to identify their conversion motif to Islam. I considered it a suitable model for this research because it is very helpful in categorizing the various reasons that were indicated in the participants' data regarding their conversions to Islam.

---

9. Table adapted from Lofland and Skonovd, 375.
10. Lofland and Skonovd, 383.

CHAPTER 2

Literature Review

Introduction

This chapter provides a brief introduction to the Igbo people, an overview of previous research on religious conversion and, in particular, Christian conversion to Islam. It examines interdisciplinary perspectives of religious conversion, conversion motifs, Islamic understanding of the phenomenon of conversion, as well as factors that influence religious conversion.

A Brief History of Igbo

The Igbo people inhabit southeastern Nigeria. Igbo refers to both the people and their language. The Igbo comprise one of the largest three ethnic groups in Nigeria. They speak the Igbo language, different dialects of which are spoken in many different localities. The Igbo are a sedentary, agricultural people and are bordered by Igalas and the Tvs to the north, the Ijaws to the southeast, the Efiks and the Ibibios to the east, and the Binis to the west.[1] The Igbo are said to "constitute the second ethnic majority in Nigerian population and are among the most numerous ethnic nationalities in sub-Sahara Africa."[2] According to the CIA's *World Factbook*, the Igbo population is estimated at

---

1. Nnadozie, "African Indigenous Entrepreneurship," 49–80.
2. Manus, "Concept of Death," 41–46.

thirty-two million people. The Igbo are the most populous Christian region in Nigeria, in fact, they are known as the "Christian Heartland in Nigeria."[3]

Culture

E. A. Ayandele described the Igbo as "a self-reliant, self-contained, incorrigibly insular, independent and blissfully tradition-encrusted people."[4] They are an industrious people, dynamic, adaptable, nationalistic, and uniquely inclined toward business and education. Emmanuel Nnadozie buttressed this further in his work on the factors responsible for the resurgence and growth of Igbo entrepreneurship during the Post-Biafra period. According to him, "The Igbos believe in hard work, enduring hardship, the spirit of sacrifice, and posterity. It is well known that the Igbo will deny himself or herself of the bare essentials to provide education for his child or children."[5]

The Igbo are industrious and enterprising, which is reflected in the effort they put into trade, business, and other professions they pursue. Prior to the European conquest of Igboland, the Igbo were engaged in the slave trade, a lucrative business that increased wealth and prestige. The abolishment of this trade led to protest and war against the British rulers by the Igbo, who eventually lost. However, the collapse of slave trade birthed Igbo engagement in trade of oil and the palm kernel in a bid to keep up with the changing rule of British masters. Rather than resist the British masters completely, or succumb to them, the Igbo pursued the acquisition of the same power and authority of their colonial masters via education as an avenue to prestigious white-collar jobs and administrative positions in the native authority system.[6]

Ottenberg rightly describes Igbo as "probably most receptive to culture change, and most willing to accept Western ways, of any large group in Nigeria."[7] Ottenberg's statement is quite opposed to Ayandele about the Igbo when Ayandele stated that the Igbo are "tradition-encrusted." Neither author is Igbo, but Ottenberg's long-standing and in-depth anthropological work among the Igbo gives him a better understanding of the Igbo. Therefore, his

---

3. Uchendu, *Dawn for Islam*.
4. Ayandele, "Collapse of 'Pagandom' in Igboland," 125.
5. Nnadozie, "African Indigenous Entrepreneurship," 61.
6. Isichei, "Ibo and Christian Beliefs," 121–134.
7. Ottenberg, "Ibo Receptivity to Change," 130.

statement about Igbo receptivity to change as opposed to Ayandele's being "tradition-encrusted" is more acceptable. Other Igbo scholars, like Elizabeth Isichei, confirm Igbo receptivity to change over being "tradition-encrusted." Their receptivity to change is observed in their rapid turn from "their traditional forms of wealth and prestige – the accumulation of yams and cowries, the purchase of titles – to the evidently superior techniques, wealth and might of the white man."[8] Their traditional forms of wealth included the slave trade, which they abandoned after its abolition and moved on to the palm oil business, and then to assimilating European products like firearms and education. Isichei further points out that, "the same emphasis on competitive achievement, which had led the Igbo to struggle to accumulate the wealth to take a title, or to grow sufficient numerous and excellent yams for a yam title, was easily transposed to education."[9] All these changes by the Igbo were possible due to the openness of Igbo culture and their receptivity to change. Ottenberg explains it this way:

> Igbo culture can then be characterized by its emphasis on individual achievement and initiative, alternative prestige goals and paths of action, a tendency toward egalitarian leadership, considerable incorporation of other peoples and cultures, a great deal of settlement and resettlement of individuals and small groups, and considered cultural variation.[10]

Individual achievement stressed in Igbo culture propels them to work hard to accumulate wealth, via trade or white-collar jobs, that is required to earn prestige, respect, and titles in society. It is a society where positions of prestige, leadership, and authority can be highly achieved by anyone. This epitomizes the Igbo belief that "the world is a marketplace, and as such, it is subject to bargain."[11] The individualistic nature of the Igbo is explained vividly by Ottenberg when he posits:

> The Ibo are a highly individualistic people. While a man is dependent on his family, lineage, and residential grouping for

---

8. Isichei, "Ibo and Christian Beliefs," 130.
9. Isichei, *History of the Igbo People*, 167–169.
10. Ottenberg, "Ibo Receptivity to Change," 141.
11. Uchendu, *Igbo of Southeast Nigeria*, 17.

support and backing, strong emphasis is placed on his ability to make his own way in the world. The son of a prominent politician has a head start over other men in the community, but he must validate this by his own abilities.[12]

This individualism offers everyone equal opportunity to enhance his status and acquire more prestige or titles through hard work, as they delve into businesses considered suitable. This is possible due to the loosely structured or flexible Igbo culture. The cultural value of Igbo individual achievement was reinforced and further heightened and expanded via cultural contact with the European cultural value of competition, which added a new dimension to the individualism of the Igbo culture. There has been an expansion into other trade markets since the cessation of the slave trade, such as migration to other territories, opportunities for white-collar jobs and increased education. These all opened up fresh avenues of achieving prestige and more deeply engrained the Igbo pattern of individualism.

The Igbo are not only keen for individual achievement, but also for individual status, which Victor Chikezie Uchendu succinctly portrayed:

> The Igbo lay a great emphasis on individual achievement and initiative. There are no restraints, human, cultural, or supernatural, which cannot, theoretically, be overcome. The individual's "bargain" for his status goal begins with *ebibi* and continues through reincarnation. When a soul makes a choice which determines his "fate," a fate which he is able to "manipulate" to his relative advantage if things do not go well for him on earth . . . The society offers alternative prestige goals and paths to fame.[13]

The ambition for achievement and status propel the Igbo toward hard work, determination, resilience, and persistence. Nothing is considered unachievable or unrealistic, so when one business fails, you try another until you discover your destiny, where you succeed and prosper. Failure is unacceptable among the Igbo people. Nnadozie portrays the Igbo unacceptability of failure like this:

---

12. Ottenberg, "Ibo Receptivity to Change," 136–137.
13. Uchendu, *Igbo of Southeast Nigeria*, 103.

Failure is a much-loathed word among the Igbos. Extensive searching for independence leads to the pursuit of financial independence as a way to escape the control of others. There is also the inner pressure to be noted, respected, and honored, coupled with the great importance attached to wealth, power, prestige, recognition, and achievement in Igbo tradition.[14]

It is important to note that the Igbo are highly communal, despite their individualism. Their sense of individualism, or better still independence, emanates from personal pride but is properly combined with a sense of communalism. "The rapidity with which the Igbos recovered from the civil war, and built churches, schools, and hospitals despite federal government neglect, confirms this sense of communalism and clearly buttresses this collectivist approach to dealing with problems."[15]

Hospitality is also a treasured attribute among the Igbo people of Nigeria:

> The Igbo are nothing if not hospitable. To them hospitality is a major social obligation. Inability to meet it is a humiliating experience for the Igbo. The general complaint of farmers after the planting season concerns the scarcity of yams with which to feed their guests. Their own need for yams, even when most pressing, is seldom discussed . . . But unwillingness to meet the demands of hospitality is another matter: it leads to loss of prestige. The inhospitable person is called many names (none complimentary) . . . In Igbo estimation, he is an unsocialized "person with a dirty heart."[16]

This value of hospitality persists today in various forms like offering of kola nut (*oji*), which signifies acceptance and welcome of the guest. There is an Igbo adage associated with giving of kola nut; *onye wetara oji wetara ndu* (whoever brings kola, brings life). "For the Igbo, giving of kola nut to one's guest signifies acceptance of that guest."[17]

---

14. Nnadozie, "African Indigenous Entrepreneurship," 65.
15. Nnadozie, 69.
16. Uchendu, *Igbo of Southeast Nigeria*, 71.
17. DomNwachukwu, *Authentic African Christianity*, 39.

The Igbo are an equally industrious group of people, which is evidenced by their actions at the end of the Biafra war when all physical, social, and economic infrastructures had been destroyed during the war. The Igbo lost virtually everything, including many businesses. Surprisingly, within a few years of hard work all were rebuilt and businesses and the economy blossomed again.

> Currently, there are hundreds of small-and medium-scale Igbo-owned enterprises all over Nigeria and other parts of Africa. Igbos currently dominate the automobile parts, electronics, and clothing businesses. Igbo entrepreneurs have made tremendous strides in the transport business; consumer durables and nondurables such as clothing, medicine, and electronics; imports and exports; distribution; and major services such as gas stations, restaurants, and hotels.[18]

Igboland today is referred as the "Taiwan of Africa" due to the industrious nature of Igbo people.[19]

A word that could describe the Igbo people is entrepreneurship. Their entrepreneurial spirit and desire for achievement are inculcated in them so early that it becomes ingrained as part of their lives and culture. "In Nigeria today, the Igbo are known to live in every part of the country doing their businesses, no matter how obscure or difficult the terrain. Beyond the shores of Nigeria, many are also found excelling in their chosen vocations."[20]

Government

Central leadership is non-existent in Igbo culture, as emphasized in their proverb *Igbo enwe eze* (the Igbo have no king). In Igboland, functional kingship does not exist. The power and authority reside within the *umunna* (the kindred comprising of the first male born of every family called *okpara*) and the communities. Each community is still autonomous, and where a king is appointed, he rules the subjects through the *umunna*. E. C. O. Ilogu rightly reinforces this point:

---

18. Nnadozie, "African Indigenous Entrepreneurship," 57.
19. Nnadozie, 57.
20. Nwagbara, "Igbo of Southeast Nigeria," 108.

> There were no *Ezes* whose authority extended to very wide areas and so the Igbo did not, in the past, organize empires and kingdoms. Rather marriages, and common interests like defense against any warrior intruders, united many communities into voluntary confederations.[21]

This type of organization does not negate the presence of leadership in Igbo culture, but rather points to them being an egalitarian people; they are governed by councils of elders known as *umunna*, where members reserve an equal right to express opinions. This is another aspect of Igbo culture that aids the receptivity of the culture to change, and encourages an individual's independence.

Peter DomNwachukwu succinctly summarizes this Igbo trait that distinguishes them from other African nations and their relationships:

> The Igbo are a peculiar African nation. Unlike most of their African counterparts, they have a high sense of individualism and function as autonomous persons, both socially and politically. On the other hand, like almost all African communities, there is no clear division between religious and secular life. Life is a unity.[22]

Several factors contribute to Igbo receptivity to change: cultural value of individualism/independence, environmental, socio-cultural, political, economic, psychological, and philosophical factors. Some of these factors are inherent, while others are induced.

Igbo Traditional Religion

Traditionally, the Igbo are inherently religious. Their religiosity permeates into every ramification of their lives, "Among *Ndi Igbo* (Igbo people), religion is integrated into the political, social and economic lives of the people; religious beliefs have control over many aspects of the people's lives."[23] Arthur Leonard, quoted by T. Uzodinma Nwala, supports the idea of Igbo religiosity

---

21. Ilogu, *Christianity and Igbo Culture*, 14–15.
22. DomNwachukwu, *Authentic African Christianity*, 203.
23. Amadi, *Curriculum Materials*, 42.

by detailing the deep-seated root of religion among the Igbo, and noting how it influences their daily lives:

> they (Igbo) are . . . a truly religious people of whom it can be said, as it has been said of the Hindus, that they eat religiously, drink religiously, bath religiously, dress religiously, sin religiously . . . Religion of these natives is their existence and their existence is their religion.[24]

The Igbo worldview reflects a two-tiered world, the material world, and the immaterial world of the spirits, just like some other African cultures. The material world is "peopled by all created beings and things, both animate and inanimate"[25] while the immaterial world "is the abode of the creator, the deities, the disembodied and malignant spirits, and the ancestral spirits."[26] There exists reciprocal expectation and mutual obligation between the two worlds and the objectives are "to ensure peace and prosperity for the people, and the survival of their lineages through time."[27]

Igbo primal religion is such that it can be reinterpreted, redefined, and manipulated to suit the desire of the Igbo. It does not hold rigidly to a single paradigm or set of assumptions, but instead draws upon multiple ideas. In fact, Igbo primal religion is an anthropocentric religion. Igbo, like other African people, believe that the goal of religion is salvation, understood as viable life, better life, and higher social status. This viable life includes "all that makes for status and prosperity, together with bodily health, multiplicity of children, fertility of land, as well as the tranquility of order within society and nature."[28]

The Igbo expect to receive viable life from religion and any religion that fails to provide this is discarded. So, the Igbo expect power for better life to stem from religious commitment. This is illustrated in the Igbo proverb, "When we offer sacrifices to whomever the gods are, they should reciprocate by performing their duties. And if the gods become overbearing, we shall show him the tree from which it was carved." They equally discard any god,

---

24. Leonard quoted in Nwala, "Igbo Philosophy," 144.
25. Leonard quoted in Nwala, 144.
26. Nwagbara, "Igbo of Southeast Nigeria," 130.
27. Ubah, "Religious Change among the Igbo," 71.
28. Okorocha, *Meaning of Religious Conversion*, 130.

minor or major, or religion that fails to yield this viable life, for another more powerful one that provides it. It was this power for viable life that resulted in their conversion to Christianity. This is why Cyril C. Okorocha refutes the popular claim that Igbo conversion is socio-economic. It also affirms Robin Horton's "intellectualist theory," which explains that

> the acceptance of Islamic and Christian beliefs and practices are only accepted where they happen to coincide with responses of the traditional cosmology to other, non-missionary, and factors of the modern situation. Where such beliefs and practices have no counterpart in these responses, they tend to be weakly developed or absent from the life of converts. Again, where responses of the traditional cosmology to other factors of the modern situation have no counterparts in the beliefs and practices of the world religions, they tend to appear as embarrassing additions to the life of converts.[29]

This same expected goal of religion (viable life) is reflected in the conversion motif of Western Toba Hunter-gatherers to Christianity:

> besides their (missionaries) role in evangelization, the missions offered various services – such as food, schooling, and healthcare – that effectively attracted the bands. The stations also offered to the indigenous people a safe haven from the violence generated by colonizers and soldiers. The foragers were initially more enticed by the practical advantages of a mission than by the Christian theology preached to them. To many hunter-gatherer societies, their contact with missionaries (was) followed by the traumatic impact of epidemics and diseases. Shamans and healers were often unable to counteract the devastating effects of these epidemics, a failure that, in turn, emphasized the people's sense of social and cultural crisis.[30]

This same search for viable life may explain some Igbo Christians' change, or conversion, to Islam. They may have observed in Islam that power for a viable life is in greater proportion than in Christianity. Perhaps there are

---

29. Horton, "African Conversion," 104.
30. Mendoza, "Converted Christians," 200–201.

unmet expectations or needs in Christianity that are being met in Islam. Anthony Wallace's theory of revitalization explains this behavior; people abandon cultural techniques for satisfying needs, in favor of a more efficient technique that does not only satisfy the needs of the previous techniques, but also satisfies other needs the first technique could not.[31] Rebecca Norris Sachs furthers this point when she writes that a convert,

> having acknowledged something in a religion that answers an inner need, the convert then, only after discovering that this is the "right" tradition precisely because it corresponds to something already existing, begins the process of assimilating the beliefs and practices of the adopted religion.[32]

Paloutzian, Richardson, and Rambo explained what this need is, "needs for meaning, belonging, identity, and definition and commitment to a religion is a way to meet them."[33] These Igbo Christian converts to Islam may have found answers to their inner unmet need in Christianity.

The Igbo rejected Islam in the past because Islam did not present a viable life. The Muslim missionaries were "small scale traders"[34]; uneducated and financially lower than the Igbo themselves, they were trying to convert the Igbo to Islam. They could not build any schools, like the Christian missionaries who established schools in villages throughout Igboland. Today, the case has been reversed because there are several schools and institutions in Igboland established by Muslims. There are affluent and educated Igbo Muslims in Igboland. There are Igbo Muslims studying abroad who have built gigantic houses in their new home countries. In fact, becoming a Muslim in some parts of Igboland (e.g. Afikpo) ushers one into the viable life (enhancement of life and status). Today, there are several benefits of becoming a Muslim in Igboland, among which are scholarships to study in Saudi Arabia, Sudan, Egypt, etc. There is a monthly monetary allowance for Igbo converts to Islam,[35] and betterment of life. Observing this economic advantage in viable life in Islam may be drawing some Igbo Christians to Islam.

---

31. Wallace, "Revitalization Movements," 268–269.
32. Norris Sachs, "Converting to What?," 174.
33. Paloutzian, Richardson, and Rambo, "Religious Conversion," 1048.
34. Okorocha, *Meaning of Religious Conversion*, 214.
35. Uchendu, "Evidence for Islam in Southeast Nigeria," 172–188.

Another reason for the Igbo rejection of Islam in the past was how the religion was presented to them. Islam was presented to the Igbo with lots of cultural attire, which the Igbo considered unprogressive compared to Christianity, which was profitable because it enhanced their status and was seen as the key to a viable life.

> To be like the white man meant not only acquiring a new culture and up-to-date culture (the wonder of being able to speak the English language) but to have in one's hand the key to European trading firms and the desks of government offices and other white-collar jobs – symbols of the new form that salvation had assumed.[36]

This element was missing in the Islam presented to the Igbo, where they were asked to learn another language and accept a culture they perceived as unprogressive without any obvious salvation (or viable life meaning an enhancement of life and status). This element has also changed, as some Igbo Muslims retain their cultural attire, the Qu'ran is taught in the Igbo language in some mosques, and Igbo Chief Imams are fluent in the Arabic language.

This indicates that Islam now redefines, markets and adapts itself to a people's culture and worldview in order to gain adherents for itself. Clifford Geertz was so astonished at the speedy progress of Islam in Java that he expressed it "as a simple and easily marketable religious package, as has ever been prepared for export."[37] Today Islam is no longer despised in Igboland, like several decades ago. The Igbo are embracing Islam in larger numbers. The irony of this change is that the "Igbo could become all this (accepting Islam, speaking Arabic, and improved social status) without himself being changed significantly deep down inside."[38]

This equally reveals the Igbo attitude to change, they accept any system that enables them to achieve desired goals and improve their status. "The Igbos always have a preference for a system which promises better and tangible rewards. They select from the new system, those cultural traits which

---

36. Okorocha, *Meaning of Religious Conversion*, 216.
37. Geertz, *Religion of Java*, 123.
38. Ottenberg, "Ibo Receptivity to Change," 216.

can easily be reconciled with their own existing cultural patterns."[39] The Igbo attitude toward change is that of

> selective reception and reinterpretation governed by an underlying utilitarianism. Thus, the Igbo are able always to reinterpret and update values to meet new social moods, while making sure that it is always to their own advantage. They quickly discard whatever is cumbersome and out of tune with the new social tempo and go for the advantageous and attractive.[40]

No wonder Ottenberg asserts that the Igbo are the most receptive to change in Nigeria, yet they are not changing themselves. This is not only common to Igbo but to all humankind. For instance, this can also be seen in the United States of America, where more mainline denominations are declining, as many have had significant nominalism. Now more and more are identifying themselves with no religion because it is no longer necessarily socially advantageous to identify as Christian.

Igbo Cosmology

The Supreme Being

The Igbo believe in a supreme being, who is known and called by different names such as, "*Chi Ukwu* (the great God), *Chineke* (God the creator), *Obasi di nelu* (the Lord who is above), *Ose bulu uwa* (God who has the world in his hands), or *Ode n'Igbo* (the One whose Being spreads over the whole extent of Igboland)."[41] Isichei claimed that "*Chukwu* is benevolent but remote; because he is benevolent, he does not need to be propitiated."[42] I concur with this remoteness of God in Igbo traditional religion because "there is a definite belief in the existence of a Supreme being, *Chukwu or Chineke*, who is conceived as a good God, but rather far removed from us."[43] However, the Igbo demonstrate their relationship with *Chukwu* in their day to day life reflected in their worship and reverence to him. To obtain favor and success

---

39. Uchendu, *Igbo of Southeast Nigeria*, 104–105.
40. Okorocha, *Meaning of Religious Conversion*, 119.
41. Manus, "Concept of Death," 46.
42. Isichei, "Ibo and Christian Beliefs," 123.
43. Ezeanya, "Osu (Cult-Slave) System," 35.

from *Chukwu*, an Igbo must sanctify himself, obey the laws of the land and keep from shedding innocent blood.[44] Matthew O. Orji notes that the Igbo endeavor to desist from abominations that are unacceptable to *Chukwu*:

> There were many things which the Igbo termed *aru* (abomination) whenever such things happened or when they were committed by any person. Somebody could commit an abomination intentionally or unintentionally. Abomination in those days was an abomination, whether it was premeditated, done in ignorance or by an accident. Abominations were those conducts which the Igbo people felt were contrary and objectionable to the order of nature.[45]

These abominations also include "stealing yams, sleeping over a widow who still performs the funeral rites of her husband; uproot planted yams or other crops, a man sleeping over his daughter or a man sleeping over his mother or any two relatives of opposite sex sleeping over themselves."[46] Igbo reverence for the supreme being (*Chukwu*) is reflected in their names, proverbs, folklores, and speech. For instance, names such as: "*Chukwuneke* (God creates), *Chukwunyere/Chinyere* (God gave), *Chukwuma* (God knows), *Chukwumaijem* (God knows my steps or my journey)"[47] express Igbo faith, relationship and confidence in God.

This supreme being (*Chukwu*) is the creator of *Uwa*, the visible universe and everything in it, including "*uwa nkea*, the natural world, and *Ala mmuo*, the spirit world."[48] All of the spirits in both worlds derive their essence from *Chukwu* and are his emissaries. African ontology, which includes the Igbo, is all-inclusive; John Mbiti rightly explained this when he asserted that "This ontology includes God as the Originator and Sustainer of other beings; the spirits and those of men who had died long ago, including all human beings and those yet unborn, animals and vegetation, and the inanimate phenomena."[49]

---

44. Okodo, "Igbo Man's Belief," 1.
45. Orji, *The History & Culture of the Igbo People*, 145.
46. Okodo, "Igbo Man's Belief," 1.
47. Arinze, *Sacrifice in Ibo Religion*, 9.
48. Manus, "Concept of Death," 46.
49. Mbiti, *African Religions and Philosophy*, 20.

For the Igbo, there cannot be life without *Chukwu*; this belief permeates every aspect of their life and influences their relationship with fellow man.

Divinities

The Igbo believe in several divinities that include: *Amadioha* (lighting); *Igwe* (the sky); *Anyanwu* (the sun); *Ala* (the earth goddess), the custodian of the moral code and punisher of breaches in the moral code; and *Uhejioku* (yam deity), responsible for agricultural production and punishment of those who steal products of the farm, especially yams.[50] Every Igbo village had a common deity responsible for the welfare and security of the community, and who held the key for its future. Any calamity that befell the community, like a loss in war or an epidemic, were attributed to the anger or displeasure of a divinity against the community for inappropriate behavior or negligence. The deities were ascribed credit for good occurrences in the community as well, such as "victory in war, economic prosperity, and good health."[51]

The divinities judged over cases brought to them by an individual or group; the result of their judgment was obvious and immediate. For example, any oath taken on falsely would be publicly punished by the *Amadioha* (the deity), either by smiting the individual dead immediately, or infecting him or her with madness. The Igbo offered sacrifices of thanksgiving to honor the divinities during their festive seasons, for good farm produce and prosperity experienced in the community. The deities were served by priests, whose appointments were hereditary. It was ascribed to be a prestigious position so that the one chosen must not object. Failure to accept the priestly position lead to grave calamity upon the chosen individual, his family, and the community as a whole. The anger of the deity was demonstrated in a community through famine, consistent death, and drought.[52]

According to C. N. Ubah, "The major deities had sacred animals with which their names were associated. These animals were never harmed, killed, or eaten, and were believed to be absolutely harmless to people. If killed accidently, they were given ritual burial of the type normally accorded to human

---

50. Ubah, "Religious Change among the Igbo," 74.
51. Ubah, 73.
52. Ezeanya, "Osu (Cult-Slave) System," 36.

beings."[53] My childhood experience confirms this view of the role of deities. I grew up in Nkpor, Anambra State, where the community worshipped a deity known as *eke Idemili*, a mighty sacred python that must not be harmed, but rather worshipped, and who inhabited a shrine. A second experience occurred during my first missionary journey in an Igbo village called *Akaeze*, where green snakes were recognized as one of their deities (grandparents). The snakes freely crawled into people's homes unharmed; this visit was highly appreciated. A particular native who ventured into killing a green snake was made to bury the snake like a normal dead person and then he was banished from the community.

Some human beings could be equally dedicated to the more important deities at the deity's request. These people, and their descendants, were considered *osu*, a people sacrificed to the gods to assist the priests to serve the deities, or as a punishment for transgressions.[54] A person who committed an abominable crime that demanded death, might run to the shrine of a deity for protection. Though they would be spared by the community, they would be considered an *osu* and must not be touched or anyone associate with them in any way.

> Osu occupied a special area, usually around the market square where the shrine of the major deity was located. Everywhere they had their own portion of the stream and a particular section of the market for their stalls. These measures were taken to emphasis the important fact that the osu were not recognized as an integral part of the Igbo society.[55]

Isichei added additional helpful information on the *osu*: they were "dreaded and despised, dedicated to the service of a god, as were their children after them."[56] This disassociation, which will be discussed later, explains why the *osu* were attracted to the Christian gospel of human equality. The deities were feared, revered, and respected in Igbo religion as the custodians of the community. The community feared their anger, so lived according to the stipulated

---

53. Ubah, "Religious Change among the Igbo," 74.
54. Dike, "Osu Caste System in Igbo Land," 2.
55. Ubah, "Religious Change among the Igbo," 74.
56. Isichei, "Ibo and Christian Beliefs," 128.

laws governing the community to maintain justice and equity. Failure to comply attracted wrath, not just on the offender, but on the entire community.

Ancestors

Another strong traditional religious belief of the Igbo is the belief that the "spirits of departed ancestors were still interested and able to intervene in the day to day affairs of their descendants."[57] In Igbo cosmology, when a person dies they move gradually from the *Ala mmuo* (the abode of the dead) to the abode of *Ndichie* (the ancestors).[58] This is similar to other parts of Africa as reported by Mbiti, "death is a process which removes a person gradually from the *Sasa* period (now) to the *Zamani* (future)."[59] There are two kinds of ancestors among the Igbo, *Ndichie-nta* who are believed to be dead, but still living in the memories of their relatives. Mbiti calls them the "living dead."[60] When these ancestors (*Ndichie-Nta*) are finally dead in the minds of their relatives, who themselves have died, they pass on into the horizon of the *Ndichie-Ukwu* (the great ancestors). Chris Ukachukwu Manus further stressed that these ancestors are venerated "by respecting them, by giving pieces of food to them, by giving their share of kola nut each time it is broken, and by pouring out libations to them during community gatherings."[61] This practice seems to have survived in most Igbo communities, especially the sharing of kola nut.

The ancestors are considered important in Igbo traditional religion because they are still regarded as current members of the family with whom the family can still communicate via sacrifices and veneration. Most importantly, the ancestors are believed to be interceding for their relatives, protecting them, but can also harm them when they are angered by a violation of the rules that govern the family. The functions of the ancestors are similar to that of the deities, but differ in the sense that the deities look after the community while the ancestors guard over their families. Besides this function of guaranteeing good health and material possessions for the family, the ancestors are responsible for ensuring that the family does not become extinct for lack

---

57. Ubah, "Religious Change among the Igbo," 74.
58. Manus, "Concept of Death."
59. Mbiti, *African Religions and Philosophy*, 32.
60. Mbiti, 81.
61. Manus, "Concept of Death," 49.

of children. In order to maintain the posterity of the family, they (the ancestors) are reincarnated.[62]

Summarily, the Igbo traditional religion believes in a supreme god who created all other deities. However, this supreme being is remote and therefore created other deities like *Amadioha, Ala, Enu*, and others, to "cover practically every aspect of human life."[63] Prayers and sacrifices are made to them according to needs. They are sensitive to any indecent behavior or disrespect by the living, and can respond retributively to such acts. It was into such a high religiously conscious society that Christianity and Islam were introduced in Igboland.

In this section I have discussed a very brief history of the Igbo, covering their location in Nigeria, culture, and traditional religion. I have argued that the Igbo have a flexible or loose culture that makes them receptive to change. I have also argued that Igbo primal religion is anthropocentric; it can be reinterpreted, redefined, and manipulated to suit the desire of the Igbo. The Igbo, like other African people, believe the goal of religion is salvation, which is understood as viable life, a better life, and higher social status. So they easily change to any system or religion that provides this viable life, without themselves significantly changing deep down inside. In the following section, I shall trace the Igbo conversion to Christianity in order to understand how their receptivity to change, and their expectations of religion, influenced their conversion to Christianity.

Christianity in Igboland

The advent of Christianity in Igboland is attributed to two major missionary agencies: the CMS (Church Missionary Society) and RCM (Roman Catholic Missionaries, also known as the Holy Ghost Fathers). Prior to the advent of these agencies, Christianity first entered into Igboland in 1841 when the "abortive Niger Expedition, on their way to Lokoja, stopped at Abo and preached the gospel, but nothing tangible came out of this effort."[64] This first

---

62. Manus, 50.
63. Dike, "Osu Caste System in Igbo Land," 1.
64. Ubah, "Religious Change among the Igbo," 75.

introduction of Christianity is often considered inconsequential, perhaps because it yielded no immediate results.

The missionary bodies' (CMS and RCM) approach to evangelism was influenced by different missiological approaches, namely the ecclesia or institutional approach, and the people-oriented approach respectively. "The people-oriented approach stressed that the church is built through the conversion of souls, while the institutional perspective emphasized ecclesiastical or institutional establishment through which souls are won for God."[65] It was against these different missiological ideologies that these bodies carried out their ministerial activities in Igboland. P. B. Clark, affirming the ministerial ideologies, wrote:

> The Roman Church's approach to evangelization was sacramental, it was the administration of the sacraments, a ministerial function, which was all important. The Protestant approach, and this difference was born at the time of the Reformation in the sixteenth-century Europe, was fundamentally scriptural: the preaching and understanding of the "Word" was all important.[66]

However, the end goal of both agencies was to convert the Igbo people to Christianity, despite their different ideologies.

The CMS penetrated into Igboland in 1857 through Rev Samuel Ajayi Crowther (African descent). A permanent Catholic station was established in Onitsha under the leadership of John Christopher Taylor, who was a Sierra Leonean of Igbo descent. The CMS was an offshoot of the Church of England in response to John Wesley's challenge to evangelize the Nigerian interior, as well as the advocacy of Buxton to abolish slave trade. It was thought that the Christianization of Nigeria would enhance commerce and, in return, this would aid in the abolition of the slave trade.

> Let missionaries and schoolmasters, the plough and the spade, go together and agriculture will flourish; the avenues to legitimate commerce will be opened; confidence between man and man will be inspired; whilst civilization will advance as the

---

65. Nwaka, "Early Missionary Groups," 411.
66. Clarke, "Methods and Ideology," 96.

natural effect, and Christianity operate as the proximate cause, of this happy change.[67]

Education of Africans was the major mission of the CMS, which was believed to aid in the conversion of the Igbo. In order to accomplish this, they were dedicated to developing the Igbo language (written language and literacy) in order to help the people understand the word of God, adhering to their ideology that the church is built through the conversion of souls. In addition to developing the Igbo language to teach God's word, they engaged in repurchasing ex-slaves, redeeming twins, and accepting many *osu* (outcasts), rehabilitating them at the mission base. Most of the CMS mission bases were comprised of Igbo ex-slaves and *osu*, along with Yoruba ex-slaves or descendants of former slaves from Freetown.

The RCM are reported to have penetrated into Igboland in 1884 after a quarter century of CMS presence in Igboland. The RCM mission objective was to carry out "missionary activity among peoples and groups whose material and spiritual needs are greatest and who are the most neglected."[68] This was to be accomplished through the establishment of ecclesia or institutions as means through which souls are won for God. While the CMS missionaries were actively involved in developing the Igbo language to enable the Igbo to read and understand the Scriptures, the RCM were busy erecting schools and health centers in various communities, and teaching with the English language. Within a short time, rivalry ensued between the two agencies because many members of the CMS were defecting to the RCM due to their desire to learn the English language. Rev Buttersby of the CMS affirmed this:

> The few Igbo agents we have are much nearer being Romanists than Evangelicals. It has made my heart ache again and again to overhear conversation between them and Mr. Benett, and to think that these men are entrusted to do CMS work . . . They are so ignorant that they can easily be deceived by anything the Romanists say or show them in books. They believe the Romanists before they believe us. Because they sell them clothes and shoes and profess to be their friends against the Royal Niger

---

67. Buxton, *African Slave Trade*, 511.
68. Okwu, "Weak Foundations," 33.

Company . . . We hear they have taken the ground known by name of B. Factory, the ground the late Bishop Hill wanted for our own church.[69]

This rapid defection triggered the CMS to abandon their primary aim of developing the Igbo language in order to present God's word in a way that was appropriate to the culture, language, and context of the Igbo and instead they began establishing schools and teaching in English also. Those CMS missionaries who continued teaching in the vernacular lost their students, as parents relocated them to the RCM schools or the chiefs invited RCM missionaries into their communities to establish a school (equivalent to a church); this was detrimental to the CMS mission work. The Igbo observed the two agencies battle for survival as they belittled and defamed each other through derogatory songs, dramas or sermons, such as this example: "*Fada siri ofe onugbu tinye ya azu gbamgbam, Silemensi asara usa akpiri etinye ya ose na anya* (The Fada (RCM) cooked bitter leaf soup with tinned fish. Silemensi (CMS) with long throats came and were punished by the RCM who rubbed pepper in the Silemensis' eyes)."[70] The "bitter relations and the conviction of the one that the other was an agent of the devil"[71] negated the message of both sets of missionaries before the Igbo.

The Missionaries' Techniques

1. Schools

To carry out missionary activities in Igbo communities, permission by the powerful chiefs was required and was arduous to obtain. According to Ubah, "the approval of the chiefs had to be sought and obtained before the missionaries could begin their work. The site of the local church had to be negotiated, and goodwill of the chiefs was essential to ensure smoothness and success."[72] The missionaries gained easy acceptance from the chiefs because of the high prestige associated with the white man. To ensure the security of the missionaries, early churches were built around the palace of the chiefs. The missionaries enjoyed favor from the people because of the prestige they

---

69. Kalu, *Embattled Gods*, 94.
70. Nwaka, "Early Missionary Groups," 413.
71. Ayandele, "Collapse of 'Pagandom' in Igboland," 131.
72. Ubah, "Religious Change among the Igbo," 78.

benefited from in their close association with the chiefs. But despite this demonstrated kindness and accommodation, neither the chiefs nor the people were interested in their gospel.

To win converts, many techniques were applied, including the establishment of schools and health centers. The early missionaries had a slogan that governed their activities: "civilize in order to Christianize."[73] Both the Protestant and Catholic missionaries had erroneously assumed that Africans and their culture were barbaric, and their culture should therefore be replaced with Western culture in the process of Christianizing them. Christianization required civilization, therefore the missionaries focused on civilizing through education, which led to the establishment of schools. Initially, the freeborn Igbo were reluctant to attend the schools because they were mainly attended by the *osu* and the repurchased slaves, whom the free society had considered untouchable and obnoxious. They abhorred the idea of contaminating their children with these social outfits if permitted to attend the same schools.[74] However, when they recognized the economic power associated with education, the tide turned. The educated social outcastes had become employed as clerks, catechists, messengers and teachers, acquiring great power, which they often exploited.

> partly in self-defense, partly from ambition, many Igbos turned from their traditional forms of wealth and prestige – the accumulation of yams and cowries, the purchase of titles – to the evidently superior techniques, wealth and might of the white man. It was one more in a series of adaptations in which they reacted to the changing demands of Europe. Earlier, they had produced first slaves, and later palm oil, in astonishing quantities, and assimilated European products . . .[75]

Ottenberg explains why the Igbo responded to external influence in such a manner: the fluidity and multiplicity of Igbo culture, coupled with their emphasis on achievement and status are obvious factors. This is further supported by many missiologists, historians and scholars who attribute "Igbo

---

73. Gilliland and Kraft, *Appropriate Christianity*, 16.
74. Okwu, "Weak Foundations," 33.
75. Isichei, "Ibo and Christian Beliefs," 130.

conversion to Christianity to inter-alia, a desire on the part of the Igbos to cope with rapid cultural change by appropriating at least some of the ways of their colonizers and capitulation to the material inveiglements of missionaries."[76]

After recognizing the power associated with Christianity, they began releasing their sons to attend school. The establishment of schools and health centers were bait to draw them to Christianity, which was productive because even the chiefs went to the missionaries requesting them to come to their villages and establish schools.[77] The role that education played in the conversion motif of the Igbo cannot be over emphasized, because it was perceived as a ladder to power. In fact, the CMS missionaries decried this attitude:

> Painful to the CMS missionaries was the fact that these parents were primarily after "English education," that is high-quality literacy that would enable their children to seek the more lucrative careers outside the Church, as clerks in the civil service or as Warrant Chiefs or as Native Court clerks.[78]

This was contrary to the primary objective of the CMS missionaries for establishing the schools, which was to inculcate the ability to read the Scripture alone. The Igbo's thirst for education is reflected in their act of building schools in their villages, then hiring missionaries to come and teach their children.

2. Hospitals

Establishment of health centers and hospitals were another attractive technique employed by the CMS missionaries, which was a result of the rivalry between the Protestant and Catholic missions. It is strange to note that this strategy failed woefully among the neighboring Yoruba people, but the Igbo "went crazy" for it.[79] For the CMS missionaries, it was an attempt to attract more followers than the RCM, while for the Igbo, it was another opportunity to associate with the power of the Western lifestyle. These hospitals were being financed from overseas until the number of patients increased, then the natives were charged a small fee, which was easily paid. According to Smith,

---

76. Hale, "Debating Igbo Conversion to Christianity," 117.
77. Ubah, "Religious Change among the Igbo," 81.
78. Ayandele, "Collapse of 'Pagandom' in Igboland," 133.
79. Ayandele, 138–139.

quoted in Ayandele, "the amount of fees being 'cheaply paid' by the patients more than covered the actual working expenses of the mission – apart from the cost of European supervision."[80] This health care technique attracted the Igbo to Christianity, as expressed in the statement of Miss Elim, a CMS missionary nurse: "the manifest results of the work as a medium of evangelization have over and over again asserted themselves and been the means of opening hitherto unoccupied towns and villages to the messengers of the Gospel."[81] While it was a medium to evangelization, its expected result was truncated due to the lack of Igbo interest in their gospel; they were only interested in the physical benefits it offered them.

3. Gifts

Another evangelism technique applied was the use of presents to bribe both the chiefs and the community to Christianity. The missionaries visited families that appeared to be easily influenced by gifts and offered them gifts like clothes and towels. Gifts of "tobacco, hot drinks, helmets and clothes, or a combination of some of these, were offered to the chiefs, depending on the importance attached to a particular chief."[82] This kind gesture endeared some parents to Christianity, as they released their children to attend the church.

Igbo Response to Christianity

The Igbo people's response to Christianity and its message was initially resistance, though they still tolerated the missionaries. Their disdain for the Christian message was primarily based on the rejection and attack on Igbo traditional beliefs. Christianity claimed superiority and rejected any dialogue with Igbo tradition. Second, the missionaries' association with the *osu* (outcasts), accused witches, and some repurchased and rehabilitated slaves on their church compounds, portrayed Christianity as a religion of the social misfits. This public identification with the slaves and social outcasts made the freeborn indifferent to the missionaries, and uninterested in their message. At this time "it was only the underprivileged and outcast of society like slaves and lepers – those who had nothing to lose but their chains – who overtly

---

80. Ayandele, 139.
81. Ayandele, 139.
82. Ubah, "Religious Change among the Igbo," 80.

embraced the new-fangled religion."[83] These social misfits were enthusiastic about the gospel because it preached human equality and advocated change in the status quo.

The rivalry between the Protestant and Catholic missionaries portrayed Christianity, or the church, as a home of discord. Jacinta Chiamaka Nwaka buttresses this point, "They were also perceived as homes of discord and instruments through which socioeconomic and political status were enhanced."[84] In the neighboring country of Togo, the church was referred to as "the house of battle," probably due to the severe rivalry between mission bodies. The Igbo's response to this was that of wonder and detachment which reiterated their perception of Christianity as unworthy. They equally perceived the missionaries as hypocrites, exploiters, and "liars who have come to this country in order to make money"[85] because of their coalition and association with the Royal Niger Company.

Despite this negative response to Christianity, both the freeborn and the outcasts were attracted to Christianity for different reasons, which influenced their change of attitude toward Christianity. For the later, the power and money promised through social equality, change of status quo, education and subsequent jobs (as clerks, messengers, and teachers) attracted them to Christianity. The former were attracted to Christianity because of military gain and commercial connections made through association with the missionaries. Ayandele vividly narrates this change:

> It became socially advantageous to be labeled a Christian. Communities threw away idols and professed Christianity, the hope that by so doing the British invaders would not inflict physical punishment upon them. Others began to be favorably disposed towards Christianity because it was believed that this was the best way to court and enjoy the favor of the new British rulers who were known to favour this religion. Yet others became Christians because it was believed that they would thereby be rescued from the tyranny of the notorious Warrant Chiefs.[86]

---

83. Ayandele, "Collapse of 'Pagandom' in Igboland," 129.
84. Nwaka, "Early Missionary Groups," 413.
85. Okwu, "Weak Foundations," 42.
86. Ayandele, "Collapse of 'Pagandom' in Igboland," 129.

F. K. Ekechi argues that British imperialism and exploitation were the major factors involved in the Igbo conversion to Christianity: "The adoption of the Christian religion, especially by the male adults, may be seen as a clear method of adjusting to the new colonial regime in which Christianity offered visible social advantages."[87] Despite these artificial motivations for Igbo conversion, some of them embraced Christianity due to the miracle encountered during a personal disaster. Some tried their traditional divinations, prayers and sacrifices with little or no success, so they turned to the white man's god in their disillusion. A missionary quoted by Isichei illustrates it this way: "We again and again, here, in and around Onitsha, come across men and women who had paid sums of money, and offered sacrifices to their gods, on account of some child of theirs who they wished to keep alive, but who have forsaken heathenism and come to Christ on the death of the child."[88] The conversion of a native doctor further buttresses this, "The Igbo of Aguleri, on the other hand, a *dibia* with the highest titles of his town, was a man who had everything to lose and nothing to gain by becoming a Christian. A polygamist, he dismissed all his wives but one, and lived a life of extraordinary fervor until his death."[89]

From the above issue, we can observe how Igbo conversion to Christianity changed their attitude. To some, like in the case of the polygamist mentioned above, his route to attitudinal change was the *central route*, it is "the person's careful and thoughtful consideration of the true merits of the information presented in support of advocacy."[90] While that of the former was a *peripheral route* which was stimulated "as a result of some simple cue in the persuasion context (e.g., attractive source) that induced change without necessitating scrutiny of the true merits of the information presented."[91] This explains why some conversions lasted while others were temporal.

> For example, if someone accepts a religion after in-depth analysis of the religious alternative (i.e., central procession), then more deep-seated and durable, long-term changes ought to occur,

---

87. Ekechi, "Colonialism and Christianity," 103.
88. Isichei, "Seven Varieties of Ambiguity," 217.
89. Isichei, 131.
90. Cacioppo and Petty, *Attitudes and Persuasion*, 25.
91. Cacioppo and Petty, 25.

and these should be evident at one or more level(s) of personality.... This suggests that such effects due to central processing (central route) would most likely be evident in relatively stable changes in goals, behavioral adaptations, and identity. On the other hand, if one adopts a religion without carefully analyzing the information with which the person was confronted (i.e., peripheral processing (route), then it should be more manipulable by situations, easier to change, and more volatile.[92]

It is most likely that their conversion to the Christian faith was peripheral, which may explain why Igbo conversion to Christianity is debated today.[93] In fact, even missionaries acknowledged this when they described the few Igbo converts as "bread-and-butter Christians, a mere handful of men and women who were looked upon as offscourings of the land who accepted baptism as a means of improving their social image without any spiritual commitment to the new faith."[94] But in the end, a good number of Igbo accepted Christianity for various reasons.

A good case study is the *osu* dedicated to the deities, considered untouchable and isolated from the community. They were the first group of Igbo available to the missionaries and enthusiastically converted to Christianity based on the human equality message preached, which was lacking in their society.

Some of the warrant chiefs, like Chief Osuala Ndiribe of Isunjaba, along with his team, traveled to the mission stations to invite missionaries to his own town to build churches and schools. This invitation to Christianize his people was a sign of progress, and an attempt to bring development to his community like that he had seen come to other communities. The driving factor was the development of his people, as he saw the power of transformation associated with Christianity.

The conversion of Alexander Obueche of Issele is amazing. He was a leading chief, a polygamist, a wealthy blacksmith, sculptor and *dibia* (diviner). "He entered a Catholic church out of idle curiosity, and was electrified by a

---

92. Paloutzian, Richardson, and Rambo, "Religious Conversion," 1070.
93. Hale, "Debating Igbo Conversion to Christianity," 116–135.
94. Okwu, "Weak Foundations," 41.

sermon on hell. He too was converted, and led a life of such piety and charity that when he died four years later, the missionaries acclaimed him as a saint."[95]

From literature reviewed so far, Igbo conversions to Christianity were based on desired western education, socio-economic development, and protection from colonial rulers which is described by DomNwachukwu thus, "Many who came under the influence of the missionaries paid lip-service to the 'foreign faith' and stayed superficially committed because of its development-oriented appeals."[96] Despite this general view of Igbo conversion to Christianity being superficial, I am of the opinion that there are still those who genuinely converted to Christ as the experience of the notorious *dibia* above portray.

I have traced above the emergence of Christianity in Igboland and the Igbo's early response to the religion. The Igbo's quest to escape the crush of the colonial masters; desire to gain the power associated with becoming a Christian, via education and conversion; desire for status quo and achievement; receptivity to change; as well as salvation i.e. viable life (the goal of religion), were some of the factors that influenced Igbo conversions to Christianity. Ottenberg reiterates this point again, asserting that:

> The Igbo have been very willing to change, to adapt to new situations, being enterprising, and, in so doing, have given up much of their culture – their indigenous religions and rituals, their masquerades and other traditional arts as well as material culture objects – excepting their language, and their particular forms of social relationships.[97]

However, there were some Igbo who were purely interested in the gospel, whose conversions were not influenced by the afore mentioned factors. A good illustration is the conversion of the wealthy blacksmith and *dibia* (diviner), Alexander Obueche of Issele.[98] Whatever system or religion that provides viable life was welcomed. The mass conversion of the Bajju people to Christianity affirms this postulation, "factors which motivated the Bajju to adopt Christianity include oppression by the Hausa-Fulani Emirate and

---

95. Isichei, "Seven Varieties of Ambiguity," 218.
96. DomNwachukwu, *Authentic African Christianity*, 3.
97. Ottenberg, "Thoughts on Islam," 28.
98. Isichei, "Seven Varieties of Ambiguity," 218.

the colonial administration . . . opportunities for education and advancement offered by missions and churches."[99]

These factors may also explain why, currently, increasing numbers of Igbo are moving to Islam; it meets their yearnings. If this is so, can we truly claim that Islam is growing in Igboland when the adherents are not really committed to the tenets of the religion? For any religion to truly transform the African in general, and the Igbo in particular, it must "embrace his language, thought patterns, fears, social relationships, attitudes and philosophical disposition."[100] Except if this occurs, the Igbo may remain only superficially attached to Christianity or Islam. However, their superficial attachment to either religion, over time, may lead to orthodoxy within the religion or a total break to a different religion.[101] The findings of this study will enable us to better understand why some Igbo are converting to Islam. Is their receptivity to change, including cultural change, and their 'viable life' goal of religion still influencing their conversion to Islam?

The Igbo and Islam

Among Igbo scholars, there abound hot debates on when Islam penetrated Igboland. Abdur Rahman I. Doi asserts that it was during a nineteenth-century event, some others pre-date it before the nineteenth century, while Egodi Uchendu argues it is a twentieth-century phenomenon.[102] Peter Mbah argues that the spread of Islam in Nigeria through the Sokoto Dan Fodi jihad of 1804 trailblazed the penetration of Islam into areas previously untouched by Islam.[103] However, he argues that the penetration of Islam into Igboland did not follow this pattern. According to him, Islam penetrated into Igboland through a "persuasion and absorption process."[104] He claims that Islam grew gradually and was sustained in Igboland, basically through cultural circumstances and colonial state reinforcement. The religion grew during the colonial

---

99. McKinney, "Bajju of Central Nigeria."
100. Mbiti, *African Religions and Philosophy*, 3.
101. Baer, *Honored by the Glory of Islam*, 15.
102. Doi, *Islam in Nigeria*; Uchendu, "Evidence for Islam."
103. Mbah and Okonkwo, "Trade, Islam, and Politics."
104. Mbah and Okonkwo, 1.

period through trade and then the colonial state perceived Islam as a ladder to colonizing the country.

Okoh, quoted by Mbah, posits that "the earliest attempts made to establish Islam in Igboland were in the 19th century, when the Igala/Hausa Muslim traders gained inroads into the area of Nsukka."[105] This suggests that Islamic penetration into Igboland began during the nineteenth century through trade between the Igala/Hausa Muslims and the Nsukka area Igbo. However, E. Afigbo differs from this position; he opines that Islam was already present in Igboland prior to the Igala/Hausa contact with the Nsukka Igbo, "The contact between Nsukka and Igala, however, preceded the rise of Igala power as it was not just or even primarily, a question of power politics."[106] A native chief imam of Enugu Ezike, quoted by Uchendu, confirms this postulation:

> Islam came to Nsukka area around the eighteenth century. That was before the arrival of the Europeans or Christian missionaries. The people they came into contact with belonged to the Igbo religion. Those who came with this noble message of Allah came for trade or Sufism. Certainly that was not primarily aimed at propagation.[107]

Doi is widely cited by those who claim the nineteenth century of Islam penetration in Igboland because of his position on the nearness of Igala Idoma as well as the trade routes that connected them during the nineteenth-century period.

> Approximately one hundred miles long by forty miles wide, Nsukka division encompasses important trade routes which have increased contacts between Nsukka Ibos and other peoples to the north, east and west. It was from these trade routes that Islam began to penetrate through the traders . . . Islam first started in Iboland in the Ibo-Eze division near Nsukka and the first place where a substantial number of Muslims settled, practiced Islamic teachings, and built mosques was Ibagwa-Nkwo, only five miles from Nsukka. The Igala Muslims came to this

---

105. Mbah and Okonkwo, 3.
106. Afigbo, "Nsukka Communities," 1–26.
107. Uchendu, "Evidence for Islam," 173.

> area ... The Hausa-Fulanis and Nupe Muslims had established trade contacts with these areas much earlier than this, but the Fulani Jihad of Shehu Uthman Dan Fodio gave them greater enthusiasm to spread Islam. Thus Islam began to influence the Ibos in this area in the 19th century although very few Ibos accepted Islam in the early days and it did not spread any further in Iboland.[108]

Uchendu argues vehemently against this postulation stating that "Hausa presence in Igboland before 1900 was indeed rare or nonexistent in spite of the closeness of northern Igboland to North Central and Northern Nigeria."[109] She validates this assertion from Ottenberg's work which shows that before 1920 no close contact existed between the Nsukka Igbo and the northerners of Nigeria. She posits that Islamic penetration into Igboland is a twentieth-century phenomenon because the nineteenth-century-claim "challenges the historical account of the development of Islam in Igboland."[110] Saheed Ahmad Rufai set out to trace this historical account of the development of Islam in Igboland but ended up adding nothing new to the already existing literature. He relied heavily on the work of Uchendu (whom he erroneously addressed as a male throughout his work). His conclusion, based mostly on secondary data, agrees with Uchendu's findings. He concludes

> that Islam spread to Igboland through the contact of some Igbo merchants with their Nupe and Hausa-Fulani Muslim counterparts in early twentieth century. It is equally derivable that the religion did not make much progress in terms of its acceptance by the indigenous people of the area most of whom saw the religion as an alien practice among them.[111]

Nevertheless, Rufai's ability to trace the historical development of Islam in Igboland based on the existing scholarly work is noteworthy. It is a very handy material on the quick history of the development of Islam in Igboland.

---

108. Doi, *Islam in Nigeria*, 167.
109. Uchendu, "Evidence for Islam," 177.
110. Uchendu, 177.
111. Rufai, "Foreign Faith," 137–154.

According to Uchendu, three categories of persons were involved in introducing Islam into Igboland: a Muslim of Nupe origin, known as Ibrahim Aduku, who was adopted into Igboland by the Amufie village in Enugu; the migrant hunters from Hausa land and Yoruba, who were invited by the Igbo native farmers to ward off elephants that destroyed their crops; and the Northern Nigerian soldiers, whose presence in Igboland was used to subdue them to British rule. However, she posits that "the main figure connected with the introduction of Islam into Nsukka Division was Ibrahim Aduku, a horse trader, well known by his last name."[112]

Uchendu argues that Ibrahim Aduku was the first Muslim from Amufie in Enugu Ezike because of his adoption into that community. As an adopted son, he possessed equal rights as every son from the Igbo community. I differ from her at this juncture. According to her argument Aduku was a Muslim from Northern Nigeria, who was escaping the war escalating in his land. He did not join the Enugu Ezike people without religion; he was already a Muslim prior to his adoption. Though he naturalized, he is still not considered to be an authentic Igbo man. To date "some persons in that community regard him as the foreigner who settled and raised his family there."[113] Additionally, the community adopted him for a selfish purpose. He was adopted in order to represent the community before the British, with the intension that any negative repercussions should befall a stranger rather than a native. Moreover, the practice of all the Nupe (his people) and strangers in Enugu Ezike converging and settling at Aduku's compound, portray that they still considered him as their Nupe brother, despite his adoption. His adoption provided them free access and security to live among the Amufie people as Aduku's relatives. These facts render it moot to classify Aduku as an Igbo and the first Muslim from Igboland (Amufie).

Mbah recognized two Igbo possibilities as the first convert to Islam: Garba Okeme Abugu of Umuogodo Amufie or Ahmed Ugwuoke Oyima Ukwaba of Ibagwa Nkwo. He appears to believe an account that Ahmed Ugwuoke Oyima Ukwaba was the first Igbo to convert to Islam. These accounts were from oral interviews Mbah conducted with participants. I do not understand what influenced his claim, as it was not stipulated, nor was his methodology

---

112. Uchendu, "Evidence for Islam," 9.
113. Uchendu, 179.

clear, but I think that Ahmed Ugwuoke seems a strange possibility because his name has rarely been mentioned by Igbo scholars in this area of study as a possible first Igbo convert to Islam. Also, the man he called Garba Okeme Abugu, Uchendu calls Mallam Garba Oheme. I consider them to be discussing the same man because both agree he is from Umuogodo Amufie Enugu Ezike, and converted to Islam in Calabar. Uchendu argues against the view that Garba Oheme was the first Igbo Muslim; she is of the opinion that Aduku was the first because he was adopted by the Amufie community. Nevertheless, she assigns Garba Oheme dual status as "the first indigenous convert, and at the same time, the second Muslim from Nsukka Division."[114] In my opinion, Mallam Garba Oheme remains both the first indigenous convert to Islam and the first Igbo Muslim from Amufie. Aduku was not Igbo, despite his naturalization, as he was not Igbo by origin. Moreover, he was already a Muslim before his naturalization. Perhaps he could have been considered the first if he had become a Muslim after his naturalization as an Igbo.

Though Uchendu argued that the Hausa traders who came to Igboland did not spread Islam to the Igbo community, I find this inconsistent with Islamic practices, as observed from Islamic history. A Muslim carries his religion everywhere; in the market place, in politics, in the farm, and other places. A Muslim ought to use his position to propagate Islam wherever he finds himself. Muslims are encouraged to make requests for their religious rights when in the minority until they have it, and subdue the owners of the land. It is unlikely that the Hausa traders did not attempt proselytization, though they may not have done this during their early interaction with the Igbo in that region. Triulzi proves that though Muslim traders can come purely as traders at first, they will, with time, introduce their religion

> If the traders opened up the region commercially, they also brought a non-purchasable commodity, Islam, which was to assume an increasingly important role in local society. . . . At first, the traders, though openly professing their religion, refrained from making converts. They had come for trade only and they could not have time for marketing as well as preaching. "Yet, after they had settled for some time, the desire to educate

---

114. Mbah and Okonkwo, "Trade, Islam, and Politics," 4.

their half-Bertha children and, one may add, to introduce the commercial aspect of the Sharia code of law, created the need for fresh conversions."[115]

From the aforementioned debate, I am of the opinion that Islam was introduced in Igbo through the three categories of individuals mentioned by Uchendu: a Muslim of Nupe origin known as Ibrahim Aduku, the migrant hunters from Hausa land and Yoruba and lastly the Northern Nigerian soldiers. What I mean by "introduced to Igboland," is that the religion penetrated into Igboland through the above-mentioned persons, but the Igbo embraced the religion through fellow Igbo and not *ndi Hausa* as most believe. It was indigenous Igbo who spread the religion to other Igbo. Many indigenous and converted Igbo Muslims refute the claim that Islam was introduced to Igboland through Hausa traders or cattle-rearers, arguing that:

> My father was a Christian in those days. He embraced Islam through Nwaguiye, Ibrahim; he was the one that Islamized most Igbo people. Igbos originally didn't embrace Islam from Hausa, am telling you, if you trace the history. Ndi Igbo didn't embrace Islam from *ndi Hausa*. People like us saw our fathers in that religion already, and if you follow their own history you will see that they embraced the religion from their own people. It's a wrong, a very wrong story. Those cattle-rearers/Hausa traders don't have basic Islamic knowledge; they don't even have the knowledge at all. They don't have the basic Islamic knowledge. In fact, if you follow their own way you will never be a Muslim. They are a crude and brutal type, if not that I was born a Muslim, I would never be a Muslim based on what I see in the north.[116]

Conversion

Conversion has become complex in the twentieth century and has attracted interest from various disciplines of study. The term "conversion" has different meanings to different religions, "though it was usually thought of as an

---

115. Triulzi, "Trade, Islam, and the Mahdia," 59–60.
116. Author's interview with a Chief Imam 2015.

issue within Christianity, where the acceptance of Jesus as the only way is primary."[117] Arthur Darby Nock defines conversion as,

> The reorientation of the soul of an individual, his deliberate turning from indifference or from an earlier form of piety to another, a turning which implies a consciousness that a great change is involved, that the old was wrong and the new is right. It is seen at its fullest in the positive response of a man to the choice set before him to the prophetic religion.[118]

Though Norris Sachs agrees with Nock on conversion as "a reorientation to a new religious belief system," she adds that "the conversion occurs primarily because it corresponds with the convert's preexisting ideas or feelings about truth or meaning."[119]

Nock's definition indicates that conversion involves change, which he calls reorientation. This reorientation may not be limited to the soul of an individual, but includes their whole being (intellectual, religious, moral, and affective). "Conversion is intellectual (repent of our refusal to seek truth and knowledge), religious (repent of the refusal to be unrestricted in love), moral (repent of refusal to seek the transcendent good of the other), and affective (refusal to love as God has loved us)."[120] The reorientation does not only affect the soul of an individual, but his whole being. Orji buttressed this assertion vividly,

> this means in essence that religious conversion is not simply a process of becoming, . . . but a total and radical reorientation of one's life to God (not religion), that one surrenders, not only oneself, but also one's unadmitted deepest pretense to absolute personal autonomy. Religious conversion helps one embrace what is good, true, noble, and truly humanizing. It is a yes to the mystery of God that finds practical expression in love of one's

---

117. Bryant and Lamb, *Religious Conversion*, 2.
118. Nock, *Conversion*, 7.
119. Norris Sachs, "Converting to What?," 171.
120. Orji, *Ethnic and Religious Conflicts*, 59.

neighbor, ensuring that one loves unconditionally the way God would have us love.[121]

Orji's definition seems to align with my usage of transformation because it involves taking a new way of life, which is termed "total and radical transformation." Taylor concurs with Nock that conversion involves "turning from," but differs from him on what the individual turns from and turns to. Conversion, Taylor argues, simply means "moving away from an inferior to a superior tradition (in the eyes of the convert and of those in the receiving tradition, but not in the eyes of the giving tradition)."[122] Taylor's definition sounds good, but its weakness is found in what the converter moves into – a tradition they consider superior. The word "moves" does not imply a reorientation. James William captures certain aspects of conversion in his definition:

> To be converted, to be regenerated, to receive grace, to experience religion, to gain an assurance, are so many phrases which denote the process, gradual or sudden, by which a self, hitherto divided, and consciously wrong inferior and unhappy, becomes unified and consciously right, superior and happy, in consequence of its firmer hold upon religious realities.[123]

The strength of James's position is that a divine encounter is needed to bring about moral change, which is not reflected in Nock's nor Taylor's definitions. There are divine and human sides of conversion which "calls for passive and active conversion."[124] One the one hand James's definition could be brought into question as some may say that the conversion process itself is an unconscious one, and so is not entirely done "consciously" as such. On the other hand, conversion for some does also involve a deliberate and conscious process. Marc David Baer demonstrates this point succinctly:

> I argue that conversion is a decision or experience followed by a gradually unfolding, dynamic process through which an individual embarks on religious transformation. This can entail intensification on belief and practice of one's own religion,

---

121. Orji, 54–55.
122. Bryant and Lamb, *Religious Conversion*, 36.
123. James and Bradley, *Varieties of Religious Experience*, 186.
124. Malony, "Conversion," 69.

moving from one level of observation to another, or exchanging the beliefs and practices in which one was raised for those of another religious tradition. In both cases, a person becomes someone else because his or her internal mind-set and/or external actions are transformed.[125]

Religious conversion "is a complex, multifaceted process involving personal, cultural, social, and religious dimensions."[126] Lewis R. Rambo confirmed this when asserting that "While conversion can be triggered by particular events, for the most part, it takes place over a period of time."[127] There is no right or wrong process in conversion and "no single definition of conversion is either desirable or possible."[128]

Historians earlier perceived religious conversion as a gradual event, but recently extended their scope of understanding to include an instantaneous and sudden event as well.[129] Though conversion can be both gradual and instantaneous, most conversion scholars argue it is more of a gradual process than it is sudden. Historians argue that conversion is not totalizing or complete. This means that no conversion is completely total because the person converting to a new religion might convert to a different belief and practice while still holding some of their old beliefs and practices. Baer discussed four ways historians describe conversion: acculturation, adhesion (or hybridity), syncretism, and transformation (with a turn to piety).

For the purpose of this research, I define conversion as change from one religion to a different religion. As a Christian scholar, this change involves turning to Christ by faith, in repentance, and turning away from wrong lifestyle. This change may just be adhesion (accepting the outward duties of the religion, but not the spirit), but with time, this change could lead to intensification of beliefs and practices of the newly chosen religion, or lead to breaking away into another new and different religion altogether. This may sound like conversion leads to conversion; that is exactly what it is. This is why historians argue that conversion is not completely total because the person

---

125. Baer, *Honored by the Glory of Islam*, 13.
126. Mendoza, "Converted Christians," 205.
127. Rambo, *Understanding Religious Conversion*, 165.
128. Glazier, "'Limin' wid Jah": Spiritual Baptists," 155.
129. Baer, "History and Religious Conversion," 25.

converting to a new religion might convert to different beliefs and practices while still holding some of their old ones.

Conversion: Interdisciplinary Perspectives

Conversion studies are multifaceted, complex, and dynamic so that no single disciplinary focus is sufficient to explain it. "The topic of religious conversion requires the resources of various disciplines in order to understand the multiple factors and dimensions that intersect in religious and spiritual phenomena."[130] In this section, I shall survey interdisciplinary perspectives of conversion.

Anthropology

Anthropologists of religious conversion deal with religious conversion or religious change. They "identify and analyze the main factors in the conversion process of people changing their religion,"[131] as well as "specific cultural process of change."[132] Suss and Pitzer-Reyl demonstrate how converting to a new religion affects the everyday life of the convert.

> The acceptance of a new religion leads to a considerable change of everyday behavior. A change of diet, a change of clothing style and the observation of a different rhythm in the daily routine which is now shaped by religious observances are frequently the consequences of a conversion. Turning away from the original religion causes the connection to the old culture that was shaped by this religion, to become more and more fragile.[133]

This appears to be like acculturation where the culture, lifestyle, and customs of another are completely embraced.

Anthropologist Robert Berkhofer developed a salient conversion model that "emerged from the literature on Native American religion . . . [he] analyzed three chronological conversion patterns in Native American communities between 1760 and 1860."[134] (1) Community reintegration sequence – when

---

130. Farhadian and Rambo, *Oxford Handbook of Religious Conversion*, 12.
131. Gooren, "Anthropology of Religious Conversion," 84.
132. Rink, "Interdisciplinary Perspective on Conversion," 29.
133. Rink, 29, quoting Süss and Pitzer-Reyl, *Living Faith*.
134. Gooren, "Anthropology of Religious Conversion," 86.

early missionaries successfully won a handful of natives to Christianity, but the indigenous majority "Pagan Party" pressured them into apostasy and forced out the missionaries. This action resulted in a reintegrated community. (2) Fragmented community sequence – the missionaries, despite all odds, continued and won a small majority with new social values and relationships. Thus, the Native's village split into two groups, the "Pagan-oriented Indians" (pagans), and the "White-oriented Indians" (Christians). Conflicts ensued and one was required to relocate, as the both could no longer co-exist. (3) Fragmented tribal sequence – "more missionaries arrived and more Whites settled around the reservation, the coincidence between culture, social structure, and community broke down, not only in one village as in the preceding sequence but, in many towns in the tribe."[135] To remedy this fragmentation, political organization was created on the tribal level. However, "This tribal political organization was modeled after the dominant society, with a written constitution and elected officers in a government of divided powers."[136] Berkhofer's model was not focused on the conversion process among individuals, rather it emphasized how a whole community was influenced by conversions as well as the "interaction between political and cultural factors in conversion."[137]

Horton, a British anthropologist, developed the intellectualist theory of religious conversion in Africa. His approach is, however, vigorously criticized by many scholars, including some anthropologists as well, because they see it as "being deterministic and for its faulty assumptions of African Traditional Religions, Islam, and Christianity, which he presented as generic categories."[138] He argued that the religious life in a "standard situation"[139] was centered on the lesser spirits, placing the lesser spirits first and the supreme being second in his arrangement of their priority to individuals in society. Horton commenced his theory by explaining the typical traditional cosmology of Africa. He argues that when this traditional cosmology encounters modern situations like development of commerce, communications, and economics and politics,

---

135. Berkofer quoted in Gooren, 86.
136. Gooren, 86.
137. Gooren, 86.
138. Gooren, 88.
139. Horton, "African Conversion," 101.

such developments lure a great many people away from their microcosm and set them down in a wider world. To greater or lesser extent, they confront even the stay-at-home with a weakening of the boundaries which formerly insulated their various microcosms from this wider world.[140]

I concur with Horton because modernity challenges our previous ways of perceiving and doing things; even if we reject the change, it will override us.

Relating this to the acceptance of Islam and Christianity in Africa, Horton argues that it "is due as much to development of the traditional cosmology in response to other features of the modern situation, as it is to the activities of the missionaries."[141] For him, Islamic and Christian beliefs and practices

> are only accepted where they happen to coincide with responses of the traditional cosmology to other, non-missionary, factors of the modern situation. Where such beliefs and practices have no counterpart in these responses, they tend to be weakly developed or absent from the life of "converts." Again, where responses of the traditional cosmology to other factors of the modern situation have no counterparts in the beliefs and practices of the world religions, they tend to appear as embarrassing additions to the life of "converts."[142]

It can be understood that for Horton, Islam and Christianity were only catalysts, "stimulators and accelerators of changes which were 'in the air' anyway."[143] His conclusions raised strong criticism from some anthropologists and sociologists, like Islamist Humphrey Fisher who saw them as being faulty because his assumptions didn't come to pass and were not fully representative. Despite these criticisms, I find this intellectualist theory fascinating because it helps in understanding why acculturation and adhesion were common in African conversion. It appears the beliefs and practices of Christianity were only accepted in Igboland to the extent they coincided with the traditional cosmology, and where they had no counterpart, the beliefs and practices of

---

140. Horton, 102.
141. Horton, 103.
142. Horton, 104.
143. Horton quoted in Gooren, "Anthropology of Religious Conversion," 88.

Christianity became absent in the life of the Igbo Christian adherents. Could this vacuum now be part of the reason the Igbo are converting to Islam?

By 1973 Fisher had identified his own three stages of conversion patterns in Islam: quarantine, mixing, and reform.

> (1) Quarantine – this stage is a stage of orthodoxy. At this stage there are no converts, thus, no one to bring into the Muslim community heterodox beliefs and observances drawn from his or her non-Muslim past. (2) Mixing – this stage involves people from various pagan backgrounds embracing Islam with their own traditional beliefs and practices, thereby mixing ensues. (3) Reform – this third stage occurs after a lapse of centuries when a wake of reform comes, cleansing away the mixing and bringing back a purified Islam of the quarantine stage.[144]

Fisher's mixing stage can be compared to adhesion or syncretism, where converts add new beliefs and values to their existing ones without giving them up. The reform stage seems like jihad. It appears that all actions involved in the reform state, like killing and destruction to purify the religion, are acceptable.

Relating this theory to the introduction of Islam into Igboland, the first stage "would fit the situation when cattle and other Muslim traders appeared but did not particularly try to convert individuals to Islam."[145] Islam in Igboland is entering stage two of this theory and is gaining ground, "as there are an increasing number of converts who have yet to acquire through study and practice, the full tenets of Islam."[146] Nnorom further illustrates this by pointing to an "increased number of mosques and Islamic institutions (in Igboland), growing numbers of well-educated Igbo Muslim leaders, and the obvious affluence and influence of Igbo Muslim converts in Igboland."[147] This was confirmed during my research as I interviewed several Igbo converts to Islam from various states. I was shocked by the efforts of the Igbo Muslims in propagating the religion to their family members and communities.

---

144. Fisher, "Conversion Reconsidered," 31.
145. Ottenberg, "Thoughts on Islam," 27.
146. Ottenberg, 27.
147. Nnorom, "Islam in Igboland," 16.

> Since my return from Mecca, I have been engaged in preaching Islam in our community and my people have come to like it. Many of them believe, but the problem is transportation, transporting them to the central mosque for worship which is quite a distance from our community. If a mosque is built in our village, they will embrace Islam. Islam has become known and acceptable in my village, unlike those days when they mocked me.[148]

Islam is not at the third stage anywhere in Igboland, but some Igbo and Igbo scholars are concerned that Islam may get to this stage with time. This concern is inferred from the pattern of the spread of Islam in some current day Islamic nations. A current example is the killing of non-Muslims in Northern Nigeria by Muslims in order to establish an Islamic caliphate. They are determined to reform Islam by "becoming stricter in following religious rules and behavior, as converts accommodate and learn to so behave or as the religious leaders put social, military and other pressures to induce conformity."[149]

Caroline Ifeka-Moller also refuted Horton's intellectualist theory, arguing for a socio-structural explanation as a factor influencing African conversion to Christianity. She argues that desire for white power, deprivation, interdenominational rivalry, education, literacy and knowledge of the Bible were the influencing factors responsible for conversion in Africa, with particular emphasis on southeastern Nigeria.[150] Fisher and Ifeka-Moller focused on their respective religions (Christianity and Islam) in their attempts to refute Horton's position on African conversion. An obvious observation from these arguments is that African conversions were motivated by various needs, other than deliberate decision, to reorient their worldviews and pattern their lives according to the theology of Christianity or Islam. Birgit Meyer, a German-Dutch anthropologist, observed the process of conversion to Pietistic Presbyterianism among the Ewe of Ghana in the mid-nineteenth century, which provides us an example:

---

148. Author's interview with a man from Urata, 2015.
149. Ottenberg, "Thoughts on Islam," 27.
150. Ifeka-Moller, "White Power," 55–72.

> Baptism implied that a person had to choose a new Christian – preferably Biblical – name, to reject any "connection with idol-worship," to refrain from participation in "heathen ceremonies," and to take off all *dzo* ("medicine/magic") strings and amulets... Every Sunday, congregations had to attend church punctually and neatly dressed.[151]

She concludes that "Christian religion was attractive because it offered the material means to achieve a prosperous and relative high position in colonial society."[152]

The Igbo attraction to Christianity is similar to what Meyer observed among the Ewe,

> it became socially advantageous to be labeled a Christian. Communities threw away idols and professed Christianity, the hope that by so doing the British invaders would not inflict physical punishment upon them. Others began to be favorably disposed towards Christianity because it was believed that this was the best way to court and enjoy the favor of the new British rulers who were known to favour this religion. Yet others became Christians because it was believed that they would thereby be rescued from the tyranny of the notorious Warrant Chiefs.[153]

During the colonial era, many Igbo conversions were materialistically motivated, so we could term this "adhesion." However adhesion can still lead to transformation (either intensification within the religion or move to another different religion). Today there are many Igbo Christians whose conversion has been transformative through intensification, while other conversions appear to follow an adhesion pattern.

Ruth Marshall-Fratani, a British anthropologist, developed a conversion approach from her research on conversion to Pentecostalism in Africa, with focus on Nigeria. She explored "the connection between conversion to Pentecostalism and the construction of selfhood."[154] Her analysis shows that

---

151. Meyer, *Translating the Devil*, 9.
152. Meyer, 11.
153. Ayandele, "The Collapse of 'Pagandom' in Igboland," 129.
154. Gooren, "Anthropology of Religious Conversion," 91.

> It is not so much the individualism of Pentecostal conversion which leads to the creation of modern subjects, but the ways in which its projection on a global scale of images, discourses, and ideas about renewal, change and salvation, opens up new possibilities for local actors to incorporate these into their everyday lives.[155]

Her approach emphasizes the relevance of transnational connections in the conversion process, "transnationalism offers possibilities for identification and political allegiance that may allow groups to bypass or confront the nation-state, and erode its attempts to monopolize such identification and allegiance."[156] She focuses on the conversion process but also agrees that conversion opens up new possibilities for the local actors. Where these possibilities coincide with their already existing beliefs, they are accepted and where they are in opposition, they are rejected.

Anthropologists have argued that religion is beyond "just (an) idea about the supernatural; it constitutes a theory of the world, a way of constructing reality that seems uniquely real to those who experience it."[157] Religious conversion then, involves changing more than one's religion; "to change one's religion is to change one's world, to voluntarily shift the basic presuppositions upon which both self and others are understood."[158] Buckser and Glazier argue further that "conversion is usually an individual process, involving a change of worldview and affiliation by a single person, but it occurs within a context of institutional procedures and social relationship."[159]

Anthropologist Diane Austin-Broos defines conversion as a "cultural passage . . . possibly experimental at first, it becomes a deliberate change with definite direction and shape. It shows itself responsive to particular knowledge and practices."[160] She continues to assert that "to be converted is to reidentify, learn, reorder, and reorient. It involves interrelated modes of transformation

---

155. Marshall-Fratani, "Mediating the Global," 289.
156. Marshall-Fratani, 282.
157. Buckser and Glazier, *Anthropology of Religious Conversion*, xi.
158. Buckser and Glazier, xi.
159. Buckser and Glazier, xi.
160. Austin-Broos, "Anthropology of Conversion," 2.

that generally continue over time and define a consistent course."[161] This is the sense in which I use conversion in this work; it is the reidentifying, learning, reordering, and reorienting of life, as well the changing of one's worldview and religious affiliation. Here, the author agrees with historians that conversion is not totalizing or entirely complete because "conversion does not involve a simple and absolute break with a previous social life . . . as learning anew proceeds over time and requires a process of integrating knowledge and experience."[162] This cultural passage (conversion) involves "a process of continual embedding in forms of social practice and belief, in ritual dispositions and somatic experience. Cultural passage generally, and the passage of conversion in particular, are then more than 'travel.'"[163]

Austin-Broos further asserts that "comprehensive reform of another is, in fact, an elusive goal because a cultural being can never entirely know herself."[164] In other words, a convert cannot altogether break away into a completely new religion because they are a product of their culture and it influences every ramification of life, even in the new religion. So comprehensive reform into another religion is elusive. The dual conversion of a formerly Jehovah's Witness, in the work of Reidhead and Reidhead,[165] illustrates this point:

> They follow a woman from her initial conversion to Catholicism to her subsequent decision to join a Benedictine monastic order. In both cases, her conversions (the first from Jehovah's Witness to Roman Catholicism, and the second to Benedictine monasticism) . . . Yet even as a Benedictine postulant, the subject of the study acknowledges the profound ongoing impact of her Jehovah's Witness upbringing on her understanding of religion. Despite changes in affiliation and practice, her activist approach to religion and her personal relationship with the Holy Spirit – the cornerstones of her childhood religion, have remained central to her experience.[166]

---

161. Austin-Broos, 2.
162. Austin-Broos, 2.
163. Austin-Broos, 2.
164. Austin-Broos, 2.
165. Reidhead and Reidhead, "From Jehovah's Witness," 183–197.
166. Reidhead and Reidhead, quoted in Buckser and Glazier, *Anthropology of Religious Conversion*, xviii.

This is a profound observation. Relating this to Igbo converts to Islam, their change to Islam is not comprehensive because some of their beliefs and practices as Igbo Muslims are influenced by their early Christian foundations and understanding. As an example, one interviewee informed me that, as a Muslim convert, his sole responsibility is "church work" (but he meant preaching Islam).[167] In his community and Igbo society, catechist and church teachers, as well as Reverend Fathers and Anglican priests, are seen as people involved in church work. This is how their ministries and services are perceived. As a convert to Islam, he perceives preaching of Islam to his people as church work, which is a carry-over from his Christian faith. The implication of this is that the convert is not completely out of the old religion or comprehensively into the new religion.

In conclusion, anthropology of conversion "examines the reasons and motives for cultural changes, which become obvious in the behavior of a person, and attempts to draw conclusions as to the conversion which has taken place beforehand."[168]

Historians

Historians had earlier perceived religious conversion as a gradual event but recently extended their scope of understanding to include an instantaneous and sudden event as well.[169] Though conversion can be both gradual and instantaneous, most conversion scholars argue it is more of a gradual process than sudden. Historians posit that conversion is not totalizing or complete. This means that no conversion is completely total because the person converting to a new religion might convert to a different belief and practice while still maintaining some old beliefs and practices.

Baer discusses four ways historians describe conversion: acculturation; adhesion (or hybridity), syncretism, and transformation (or turn to piety). We look at the stages of adhesion and syncretism together.

---

167. Dike, "Igbo Conversion to Islam."
168. Rink, "Interdisciplinary Perspective on Conversion," 30.
169. Baer, "History and Religious Conversion," 25.

Acculturation

Acculturation is the integration of an existing culture into the customs, habits, and beliefs of a conquering civilization. Converts change their daily private and public routine, culture, language and religious beliefs and practices to adopt another.[170] Post-colonial theory argues this kind of conversion is characteristic of African conversions. African conversions to world religions were influenced by imperialism and colonialization, where the colonial power "shaped the superstructures and infrastructures of societies, cultures, economies, and subjectivities of oppressed peoples all over the world. Conversion to various 'world' religions (especially Christianity) is interpreted as a part of the 'colonialization of the minds and spirits' of the dominated peoples."[171] The conquered peoples acculturated to the new customs, religion, practices, and lifestyle of their conquerors. This kind of conversion was both dramatic and gradual. Dramatic because once the society was conquered, they automatically assumed the religion of the conqueror, then they gradually began absorbing the customs, practices, beliefs, and lifestyle of the conqueror.

Baer and many other scholars agree that conversion is a deliberate, conscious, and decisive process where as acculturation is not, it is rather an imperialism and colonialism that forces even the minds and spirits to be colonized. Though the conversion that some predicted from African Traditional Religion (ATR) to Christianity did happen, it did not go very deep.

Adhesion or Hybridity and Syncretism

Adhesion is another part of conversion where "converts to another religion cannot or do not always wish to completely break away from former beliefs and practices, but instead continue to engage in some of them privately and despite publicly changing religion."[172] Nock throws more light on adhesion:

> There is no definite crossing of religious frontiers, in which an old spiritual home was left for a new once and for all, but to men's having one foot on each side of a fence which was cultural and not creedal. They led to an acceptance of new worships

---

170. Baer, *Honored by the Glory of Islam*, 15.
171. Rambo, "Theories of Conversion," 262.
172. Baer, "History and Religious Conversion," 28.

as useful supplements and not as substitutes, and they did not involve the taking of a new way of life in place of the old.[173]

A convert in this kind of conversion has not completely rejected the old beliefs nor completely accepted the new, rather they are standing on both sides with one leg in each. Monika Wohlrab-Sahr demonstrates that conversion to Islam in the West is syncretism and a symbolic battle. She discovered that the Islam of those who converted to Islam, according to her findings, is not the same as the Islam of migrant Muslims due to the double (cultural) frame involved in their conversion, which leads to syncretism. This double frame is "the religious, cultural, and social frame that converts turn away from, but stay related to, on the one hand; and the new religious and cultural frame that they have chosen, but with which they cannot completely merge or identify with, on the other side."[174] This is often the result of adhesion; the original religion is corrupted while the new polluted, so they end up introducing a totally new religion.

Eaton refutes the theories (religion of sword, political patronage, and religion of social liberation) used to explain Indian conversion to Islam, but claims that accretion (syncretism) and reform are responsible for the mass conversion to Islam. He illustrates how syncretism was practiced:

> Persons will identify themselves as Muslim inasmuch as they worship Allah . . . , or refrain from eating pork. Two attributes which . . . might be loosely understood as the defining features of Islam. But this by no means prevents them from participating in village propitiation of a local goddess to ward off smallpox or in joining village devotions to an *avatar* of Krishna.[175]

Adhesion does not reflect a deep-seated reorientation, religious transformation or definite crossing of religious frontiers. The old is incorporated into the new rather than the new confronting the old commitment. In fact, no behavioral and attitudinal change occurs in this kind of conversion. However, just like Fisher theorized, adhesion can lead to reform.[176] This means adhesion

---

173. Nock, *Conversion*, 7.
174. Wohlrab-Sahr, "Conversion to Islam," 352.
175. Eaton, "Approaches to the Study," 112.
176. Fisher, "Conversion Reconsidered," 32–38.

is not a static state; it can be replaced with intensification within the religion, or break away into a new religion. This may explain Igbo conversion from ATR to Christianity as well as their conversion from Christianity to Islam. In time, their adhesion state in Christianity was replaced with intensification (for some). They took seriously the Christian message and modeled their lives, worldview, behavior and attitude according to the Scripture. Whereas in time, some broke completely from Christianity to a different religion (Islam), imbibing a new faith. The question for the latter is, has conversion to Islam transformed their lives or has it only led to a different way of explaining problems in the sense of a change of paradigm? Does their conversion to Islam result in a reorientation? Are they taking a new way of life in place of the old? Are they committing themselves to the theology of Islam? Are they getting into an adhesion state again in the area of religion and later will break out into another religion with time? Or are they modeling their lives, worldview, behavior, and attitude according to Islamic theology? Syncretism emerges as a response to adhesion when the convert mixes both the old and new beliefs and practices to create a new religious synthesis.

Transformation and turn to piety

Adhesion and syncretism are not a static state; they can actually be replaced with intensification or transformation over time. Transformation is "taking of a new way of life in place of the old . . . a deliberate turning from indifference or from an earlier form of piety to another, a turning which implies a consciousness that a great change is involved, that the old was wrong and the new is right."[177] This is when converts attempt to completely break away from the past or old to the new.

> Converts turn toward a new axis or set of ideals that motivates converts to transform themselves and their environment. They reject or denounce their past and former beliefs and practices, or their indifference (in the case of revivalists), labeling them wrong when compared with a different future on a new path that is conceived as being right.[178]

---

177. Nock, *Conversion*, 7.
178. Baer, "History and Religious Conversion," 33.

Transformation can occur in two ways, either turning to piety within the religion one adheres to or exchanging the beliefs or practices of their religion with another. In turning to piety, "the person who formerly did not give more than cursory thought or attention to the theology of his or her faith or did not engage in or keeping wholeheartedly to its requirements devotes his or her mind and body fully to understanding and embracing the religion."[179]

Kraft theorized that transformation ought to result in a change in allegiance (faith commitment to God), which leads to a change in worldview and in turn leads to a change in attitudes, habits, and behavior. This type of conversion involves "a radical change of worldviews and identities, linked with conflicting, exclusive relationship towards the past and former commitments."[180] Though this kind of conversion can be both dramatic and gradual, I think it more of a gradual prolonged process as the individual has to weigh the cost or experiment with it and observe its impact on adherents before converting.

In summary, conversion means different things to different persons and disciplines. In this study I shall be looking at conversion as "change and transformation."[181]

Sociology

Sociology of religious conversion studies is "the social environment of converts and the resulting changes in their personality."[182] In essence, what are the factors within the social context of the individual that influence conversion to another belief or religion? Sociologists were earlier concerned with the micro-level factors of conversion but have broadened their perspective in the twenty-first century to include meso- and macro-level factors.[183] Wohlrab-Sahr puts Yang and Abel's mirco-, meso-, and macro-level factors differently as the why, what, how and for what purpose of a conversion. Different sociological sciences examine the why, what, how, and for what purpose of a conversion to a different religious affiliation.

---

179. Baer, *Honored by the Glory of Islam*, 15.
180. Wohlrab-Sahr, "Conversion to Islam," 353.
181. Farhadian and Rambo, *Oxford Handbook of Religious Conversion*, 32.
182. Rink, "Interdisciplinary Perspective on Conversion," 26.
183. Yang and Abel, "Sociology of Religious Conversion," 140.

Lofland and Stark's classical work provides answers to the question: why does conversion occur?[184] Their proposed model of conversion is "arguably the first authentically sociological model of religious conversion in the sense that it moves beyond a psychological conception of conversion to consider personal bonds and social networks."[185] Their model demonstrates seven factors an individual undergoes in a conversion process: (1) experience enduring and acutely felt tensions; (2) within a religious problem-solving perspective; (3) which leads them to define themselves as a religious seeker; (4) encounter the movement or cult at a turning point in their life; (5) form an affective bond (or pre-exists) with one or more converts; (6) neutralize or break extra cult attachment where, if they are to become a deployable agent, (7) they are exposed to intensive interaction. The first three factors are classified as "predisposing condition," a condition an individual must experience prior to conversion while the last factors are classified as "situational contingencies." This situation leads to conscription to the group and the acceptance of the group's worldview. Complete conversion will not occur without the situational contingencies, in spite of how predisposed the seeker may be.[186]

Yang and Abel call this disposing condition micro-level. A level where "people turn toward religion when they lack something, either an 'absolute' deprivation, such as bad health or poverty, or 'relative' deprivation, as when people in any condition subjectively feel the lack of something."[187] The individual with such deprivation easily changes their identity to another group through existing friendship or short-term friendships.

Rambo's conversion process differs slightly from Lofland and Stark's model. Rambo developed a seven stages process of conversion that also answers the question of why conversion occurs. (1) Context: "the total social, cultural, religious, and personal environment" of the potential convert. Their disenchantment with the context and availability of options can "create perplexity and alienation . . . people may eagerly choose a new religious option to lessen anxiety, find meaning, and gain a sense of belonging." (2) Crisis: this could be "religious, political, psychological, cultural, or a life situation

---

184. Lofland and Stark, "Becoming a World-Saver," 862–875.
185. Yang and Abel, "Sociology of Religious Conversion," 142.
186. Lofland and Stark, "Becoming a World-Saver," 865–875.
187. Yang and Abel, "Sociology of Religious Conversion," 142.

that provides new options. At this stage, myths, rituals, symbols, goals, and standards cease to function well for the individual or culture. Such a crisis creates great disorientation in the individual's life." (3) Quest: search for meaning and purpose in life which intensifies under crisis or abnormal situations. (4) Encounter: "involves the contact between the potential convert and the advocate and takes place in a particular setting." The outcome of the contact is influenced by "compatibility of ideology, age, sex, education, and similar attributes." The needs of both the potential converts as the advocate, as well, are included in this stage. (5) Interaction: the potential convert is exposed to "the teachings, lifestyle, and expectation of the group" through communication and social interaction. (6) Commitment: the convert declares their involvement in the new religion explicitly and publicly through "biographical reconstruction, testimony, rituals, pain induction, decision making, and surrender." (7) Consequences: the effects of this conversion on their ideas, relationships, and lifestyle.[188]

Though Lofland-Stark and Rambo differ in their conversion process, they agree on certain stages like Lofland-Stark's stage one aligns with Rambo's stage two. Three and four are the same, though others differ slightly. Lofland-Stark claim their model is "universal,"[189] but Snow and Philips, working among the *Nichiren Shoshu* Buddhist movement in America, proved them otherwise. Rambo acknowledges his model is not "universal and invariant."[190] Both authors consider the conversion process from different disciplines: sociology and psychology respectively.

Luther P. Gerlach and Virigina H. Hine developed a conversion model to explain why conversion occurs based on extensive ethnographic research among two groups, the Pentecostal and Black Power movements, in US society. They discovered seven stages involved in a person's conversion process as comprising. (1) Initial contact with a participant: A potential convert with predisposing tension converts to a new religion through personal contact with a participant in the new religion. This initial contact is achieved through their pre-existing, important social relationships. (2) Focus of needs through demonstration: This involves "redefining the potential convert's needs, desires,

---

188. Rambo, "Psychology of Conversion," 159–177.
189. Lofland, *Doomsday Cult*, 61.
190. Rambo, "Psychology of Conversion," 163.

or discontents in terms of the specific ideology of the movement."[191] At this stage, the individual observes changes, fulfillment, and satisfaction in the life of a relative or friend who joined the movement and knows that they can experience the same. (3) Re-education through group interaction: To maintain and sustain commitment, the convert must identify with the values of the movement to grow through group interaction; commitment cannot be sustained in a vacuum. If external relationships are neutral or weak, the potential convert will quickly bond with the new religion through relationships with its members. This is similar to Lofland-Stark's interaction stage. (4) Decision and surrender: At this stage, the convert surrenders the old identity and transfers control to something outside the individual's consciousness. Theologically, this is called repentance or acceptance of Christ as Savior. This is a crucial point in commitment whether the commitment was coerced or persuaded. (5) The commitment event: An event to which commitment can be traced, is in the experience of salvation (Christian circles) and the act of baptism in the Holy Spirit, which "symbolize a turning away with finality from things and people associated with one's former role which in many cases actually provide the skills and initiate the behavior patterns expected in the new social role."[192] Commitment comprises four major elements: strength of conviction, capacity for risk-taking, personal charisma, and behavioral change. (6) Testifying to the experience: a convert is encouraged or pressured to publicly share their experience with the group. "Talking about their subjective experience effectively clarifies and reifies it for the individual and draws immediate reinforcement from the group . . . and 'fixes' it as a reality, both for the convert and for his group. Without this step in the commitment process, much of the transforming effect of the commitment event would be lost."[193] (7) Group support for changed cognitive and behavioral patterns: Converts are warned of subtle satanic opposition through family and friends. Doubt as well as other psychological and physical trials are attributed to this source. Support from other members during this period is essential.[194]

---

191. Gerlach and Hine, *People, Power, Change*, 111.
192. Gerlach and Hine, 135.
193. Gerlach and Hine, 136.
194. Gerlach and Hine, 111–137.

The three scholars referenced here all developed seven stages or factors of conversion processes, which differ at some points and are parallel at others. This trio adopted different terms for each stage but are the same in the area of interaction. Rambo's is a "modification of the work of Tippet as well as Lofland and Stark's models."[195] The outstanding point in all these models is that potential converts undergo certain processes before conversion, which validates the popular claim that conversion is gradual. All these processes do not occur in a moment, rather they occur gradually as the convert considers his losses and benefits of converting.

Stages three (re-education through group interaction) and five (the commitment event) are considered very crucial in determining if a genuine personal conversion has occurred. Gerlach and Hine's model is helpful in understanding the individual conversion process, though it is combined with religious organization movements. They conclude their model, which they claim is universal, by identifying five important factors in establishing religious and social movements: (1) personal commitment, constructed along the seven factors or stages in the conversion process; (2) enthusiastic persuasion of friends, relatives, and neighbors to join in the small-scale effort; (3) articulation of beliefs and ideals appropriate to the contemporary period of national and world history; (4) building flexible, non-bureaucratic cell group organizations, which can be created, altered, or dissolved at the desire of participants; (5) expectation of and willingness to face opposition from those dedicated to the maintenance of the status quo.[196]

Henri Gooren explains how "Anthony Wallace developed a model to explain periods of accelerated cultural change by looking at the crucial role of movements like Handsome Lake, Peyote, and Ghost Dance in North America."[197] He (Wallace) expounded upon a theory that is connected to conversion, and which he labeled "mazeway;" "the mazeway is nature, society, culture, personality, and body image, as seen by one person."[198]

---

195. Rambo, "Psychology of Conversion," 163.
196. Gerlach and Hine, "Five Factors Crucial to the Growth," 23–40.
197. Gooren, "Anthropology of Religious Conversion," 85.
198. Wallace, "Revitalization Movements," 266–267.

Mazeway is crucial in the conversion process of an individual. Wallace theorized a universal model that describes stages of all revitalization movements that individuals, globally, ought to go through.

1. Steady state: A culturally recognized efficient technique for satisfying needs and reducing stress within a system that already exists. "The techniques for satisfying other needs are not seriously interfered with and abandonment of a given technique for reducing one need in favor of a more efficient technique does not leave another need, which the first technique satisfied, without any prospect of satisfaction."[199]

2. The period of individual stress: This is a point where individual members of a population begin to experience decreased efficiency in the techniques of stress reduction caused by external factors like economic distress, climatic change, epidemics, etc. They try to tolerate the inefficiency, but it gets to a point where they start considering alternatives or substitutes. The initial consideration of a substitute arouses stress due to the anxiety that the substitute may be less effective than the previous technique and because accepting the substitute may hinder execution of other ways.

3. The period of cultural distortion: At this stage, the prolonged experience of stress caused by the decrease in the efficiency of a stress reduction technique and anxiety of the prospect of substitution (or changing a behavioral pattern) are responded to differently. People with a rigid personality will continue to endure and undergo the intensified stress, while flexible people will add and substitute in order to cope or adapt to the change. The various responses (aggression or aggressive behaviors) become a new culture, the culture then becomes "internally disoriented." Finally, when the inefficiency of the techniques becomes more and more obvious and the anxiety of substituting a meaningful way of life becomes equally obvious, then disillusionment with the mazeway sets in.

4. The period of revitalization: This is the most crucial phase because the deterioration can lead to death of the society or movement.

---

199. Wallace, 265.

These movements must perform six important tasks at this stage to survive: mazeway, transformation communication, organization, adaptation, cultural transformation, and routinization.

5. The new steady state: Once cultural transformation has been accomplished and the new cultural system has proved itself viable, and the movement organization has solved its problems of routinization, a new steady state may be said to exist. The culture of this state will probably be different in pattern, organization or *Gestalt*, as well as in traits, from the earlier steady state, and it will be different from that of the period of cultural distortion.[200]

The second concern of sociologists is the question of what conversion really is. Some argue that religious conversion is a fantasy solution to stress. Others argue that it is simply socialization and learned behavior or due to interaction with a devout person. Heirich, through his work among Catholic Pentecostals and using a control sample, criticized the conventional arguments of these social scientists because "by treating it (religious conversion) as an odd experience and attempting to explain it in social-psychological terms that ignore how its *content* relates to the structure of larger patterns for social interaction."[201] Though sociology is helpful in understanding the why of religious conversion, this is insufficient in itself. Rambo provides a holistic model to understanding religious conversion, which he termed "a heuristic framework." This framework enables "a student of the phenomenon to ask a wide range of questions and explore various problems."[202]

The fourth paradigm addresses the question, for what purpose does conversion occur? Wohlrab-Sahr's research among German and American converts to Islam shows that their conversion was "a means of articulating problems of disintegration in one's own social context because it is through the adoption of the 'other' that the problem of disintegration within one's own context can be articulated."[203] Her further research in 2002 confirmed a similar purpose for conversion. "More frequently, it is crises in the personal

---

200. Wallace, 265–275.
201. Heirich, "Change of Heart," 677.
202. Rambo, "Psychology of Conversion," 48.
203. Wohlrab-Sahr, "Conversion to Islam," 351–361.

lives of the converts, (such as sexual humiliation, failed attempts to achieve promotion, or ethnic problems) the solution to which is seen in a religious frame."[204] Converts, therefore, convert hoping to alleviate their crises and troubles through conversion to a different religious faith.

Lofland and Sknovd's six conversion motifs equally answer the question for what purpose does conversion occur? The six conversion motifs are thus: (1) Intellectual: The person seeks knowledge about religious and spiritual issues via books, television, articles, lectures, and other media that do not involve significant social contacts. (2) Mystical: This conversion is characterized by high subjective intensity and trauma. It is generally a sudden and traumatic burst of insight, induced by visions, voices or other paranormal experiences. (3) Experimental: The prospective convert takes a pragmatic "show me" attitude, ready to give the process a try, but withholding judgment. (4) Affectional: This motif highlights interpersonal bonds as an important factor in the conversion process. Personal experience of being loved, nurtured, and affirmed by a group are central to the conversion. (5) Revivalist: This motif refers to managed or manipulated ecstatic arousal in a group or collective context that has transforming effects on the individual. (6) Coercive: The motif may be well explained by terms such as "brainwashing," "programming" or "mind control." The two keys in this motif are the compulsion of an individual and the confession of guilt or acceptance of an ideological system.[205]

The fourth motif, *affectional*, portrays the new group as caring, loving, and affirming toward the potential convert they desire to convert. Though they are applying social pressure, it "exists and functions more as 'support' and 'attraction' than as 'inducement.'"[206] This is noteworthy as Michael Ezra Dikki's research among Christian converts to Islam in Kenya shows the affectional motif as the reason for their conversion to Islam. This is a social pressure employed by Muslims in the form of support in order to attract Christian adherents to the religion. So the claim that "Muslims are more loving and caring than Christians," ought to be viewed as an Islamic proselytization strategy to put pressure on the individual. Their intellectual motif is what

---

204. Rink, "Interdisciplinary Perspective on Conversion," 25–26.

205. The six conversion motifs are explained fully in chapter 1, "Conceptual Framework," p. 7. See Kim and Mehmedoglu, "Conversion Motifs," 124; Lofland and Skonovd, "Conversion Motifs," 373–384.

206. Lofland and Skonovd, "Conversion Motifs," 380.

many scholars describe as the activist type of conversion. These sociological schools of thought can be complementary to each other in helping us understand religious conversion.

Psychology

Religious conversion for psychologists "initially seemed to be seen as an event, a specific moment when someone came to a point of faith."[207] This kind of conversion is considered valid only "if the person experienced a crisis that was relieved by a dramatic conversion."[208] This seems to parallel evangelical Christian understanding of conversion, with Paul's Damascus experience used as a yardstick for authentic conversion. However, we should note that there was no crisis involved in Paul's case prior to his conversion, though his conversion was dramatic. The demerit of the psychologist's position is that conversion is not only an event, but also a process that could be prolonged before an intended convert changes to another religion.

> Religious conversion provides converts with an opportunity to embrace a community of faith and a philosophy that nurture and guide that offer a focus for loyalty and a framework for action. Whether the conversion is from one religious tradition to another, from one denomination to another, from no involvement to participation in a religious community, or is an intensification of commitment within one's faith, the process can be complex but compelling and transformative.[209]

Edwin Diller Starbuck[210] focused his studies on "when conversion occurred, how it occurred, what mental or emotional states were involved at the time, prior to it, or following it, and the nature of the changes in attitude, affect, and behavior over long periods of time following conversion."[211] Starbuck, like Lofland and Stark, claims that negative psychological conditions precede conversion. For Starbuck the negative psychological state includes "a mixture of anxiety, depression, guilt, aimlessness, doubt, unhappiness, and

---

207. Paloutzian, "Psychology of Religious Conversion," 211.
208. Paloutzian, 211.
209. Rambo, *Understanding Religious Conversion*, 1.
210. Starbuck, *Psychology of Religion*.
211. Starbuck quoted in Paloutzian, "Psychology of Religious Conversion," 212.

related feelings. If this state is sufficiently intense, a person would be motivated, maybe driven, to seek a solution to the crisis."[212] Conversion provides solution to this problem because they are replaced with "positive feelings such as happiness, peace, joy, and a sense of being 'new' or 'reborn' would ensue."[213]

In conclusion anthropologists, historians, sociologists, and psychologists have grappled, and are still grappling, with defining and explaining religious conversion. This demonstrates that the conversion phenomenon is a complex one and no single discipline, model, or motif has been able to adequately explain it.

Rodney Sebastian and Ashvin Parameswaran discovered four typologies of interaction that exist between ethnic Chinese who adopt an alien faith, Hare Krishna, and their family members.[214] These are classified as contentious, neutral, accommodative, and supportive.

Contentious interaction is typified by "an all-pervading sense of anger and bitterness, which is maintained over long periods of time, between convert and family members. The convert's new religion is opposed as well and the convert resents this opposition."[215] The family members are "convinced that recruits have been manipulated at all stages of the conversion process and during subsequent involvement in the movement's activities."[216] This interaction is characterized by very high conflict and very low consensus.

In neutral interaction, the family members' reaction is non-extreme and it is characterized by low conflict and low consensus. "The family members are neutral towards the devotee's conversion and the convert is glad that s/he has at least been given enough space to do what s/he wants, while simultaneously wishing for more support."[217] Family member's neutral interaction could be a result of their insufficient knowledge about the positive or negative effect of the decision on the convert. It could also depend on the age and beliefs of the convert.

Accommodative interaction is characterized by high conflict and high consensus. In this interaction typology, the family accepts certain aspects

---

212. Starbuck quoted in Paloutzian, 212.
213. Starbuck in Paloutzian, "Psychology of Religious Conversion," 212.
214. Parameswaran and Sebastian, "Conversion and the Family," 347–350.
215. Parameswaran and Sebastian, 347.
216. Parameswaran and Sebastian, 347.
217. Parameswaran and Sebastian, 350.

of the convert's faith while opposing others. Negotiation and engagement are involved in an attempt to accommodate both the convert's faith and the beliefs of the family.

Supportive interaction is characterized by low conflict and high consensus. "The family members feel that the new religion is beneficial to the convert. Sometimes, the convert responds by preaching to his/her family member(s) and the supporter might end up becoming a devotee him/herself."[218] The kind of interaction that exists between converts and their families depends on the following causal conditions: family-convert relationship, religious identity of family member, convert's habitation, and family members' perceptions of convert's religion.[219]

Christian Understanding of Conversion

Christian conversion "involved saying yes to Jesus by means of a simple prayer of repentance and faith."[220] ". . . conversion in the Christian sense is undoubtedly a personal decision to accept the saving power of Christ and to enter into his discipleship."[221]

> Christian conversion as demonstrated in the New Testament is not about substituting something new for something old. . . . Christian conversion requires something much more radical. It is less about content than about *direction*. It involves turning the whole personality with its social, cultural, and religious inheritance toward Christ, opening it up to him. It is about turning *what is already there*.[222]

According to Peace, "Christian conversion is characterized by a decision (repentance) based on understanding (awareness, consciousness, conviction) to turn around from a life of sin (darkness, disobedience, waywardness) to the way of Jesus (light, God, holiness), with a resultant new way of living in

---

218. Parameswaran and Sebastian, 349.
219. Parameswaran and Sebastian, 350.
220. Peace, *Conversion in the New Testament*, 2.
221. Bent, "Concept of Conversion," 388.
222. Walls, "Converts or Proselytes?," 6.

the context of the Kingdom of God."²²³ When a person becomes a Christian, there must be observable behavior to that effect.

Bernard J. F. Lonergan considered conversion as self-transcendence, "the transformation of the subject and his or her world."²²⁴ Orji explains that "underneath the idea of self-transcendence is the paradox that authentic self-realization comes, not from an attempt to satisfy one's personal desires, but in seeking and bringing about the good of one's neighbor."²²⁵ Orji defines conversion as "a shift or movement into a new horizon."²²⁶ This movement into a new horizon means that the "converted apprehends differently, values differently, and also relates differently because one has affected a shift in one's horizon."²²⁷ He posits that conversion is not only an individual event, but also multi-dimensional because it brings change on personal, social, moral and intellectual levels. Lonergan discusses in detail the changes that occur in an individual when conversion takes place. They are as follows:

Intellectual conversion: Lonergan defines this kind of change as "a radical clarification and, consequently, the elimination of an exceedingly stubborn and misleading myth concerning reality, objectivity, and human knowledge."²²⁸ According to Orji,

> intellectual conversion helps one to renounce hitherto held false ideas and philosophies as one begins to conceive reality in a new and true light. Intellectual conversion is something one does for oneself. It is one's own intelligent inquiry and insights, one's own critical reflection, and one's own "personal decisive act", which Lonergan speaks of as the goal of *insight*.²²⁹

"Intellectual conversion helps to cast off false ideas and philosophies which one had imbibed for a very long time."²³⁰ This appears to be similar to Lofland and Skonovd's intellectualist conversion motif, which is acquired through

---

223. Peace, *Conversion in the New Testament*, 8.
224. Lonergan, *Method in Theology*, 130.
225. Orji, *Ethnic and Religious Conflicts*, 52.
226. Orji, *History and Culture of the Igbo People*, 52.
227. Orji, 52.
228. Lonergan, *Method in Theology*, 238.
229. Orji, *Ethnic and Religious Conflicts*, 54.
230. Igboin, "Bias and Conversion," 169.

personal diligent private investigation into new religion via extensively reading literature about the religion, attending lectures, watching television, etc. I found this fascinating because it is a disciplined enquiry one does for oneself, conversion to Christ must reflect a change at the intellectual level, meaning that the convert begins thinking differently.

Religious conversion: The second major change is religious conversion. By this, Lonergan means the "other-worldly falling in love, the grasp of ultimate concern, the total and permanent self-surrender without conditions, qualifications, or reservations."[231] Orji explains this further:

> Being in love with God does not occur in isolation from our intellect and emotional concerns. Rather it changes one's entire existence. This unrestricted love is the heartbeat of a genuine religion, sets up a new horizon, resets our values, and alters our knowing. What this means in essence is that religious conversion is not simply a process of becoming, say a Christian or Muslim, but a total and radical re-orientation of one's life to God (not religion), that one surrenders, not only oneself, but also one's unadmitted deepest pretense to absolute personal autonomy. Religious conversion helps one embrace whatever is good, true, noble, and truly humanizing. It is "yes" to the mystery of God that finds practical expression in love of one's neighbor, ensuring that one loves unconditionally the way God would have us love.[232]

Moral conversion: This "consists in opting for the truly good, even for value against satisfaction when value and satisfaction conflict."[233] Taking it further Orji asserts,

> It's a matter of deciding to act responsibly and inculcating a value-laden ethics in which one is governed by the criterion of what is truly good, as against apparent good that merely satisfies one's immediate demands for self-gratification. Thus, a morally converted person is radically attuned to seek the good of others. Or as Lonergan puts it, in moral conversion one exercises

---

231. Lonergan, *Method in Theology*, 240.
232. Orji, *Ethnic and Religious Conflicts*, 44–45.
233. Lonergan, *Method in Theology*, 240.

vertical freedom which advances one towards authenticity and makes one opt for the truly good, i.e. good of value, even when such good is in conflict with the good of satisfaction.[234]

Affective motive: The affective motive was derived from other scholars; it is "the concrete possibility of overcoming moral impotence, of not only being able to make a decision to commit oneself to a course of action or direction of life judged worthwhile or personally appropriate, but of being able to execute that decision over the long haul against serious obstacles."[235] Affective conversion "is a kind of falling in love, that part of love that is concerned with ultimate meanings and what is ultimately worthwhile."[236] One is effectively converted "when the isolation of the individual is broken and he or she spontaneously acts, not just for self, but for others as well."[237]

This change is also observable in the new lifestyle the convert adopts. Charles Harold Dodd writes, "the style is the man."[238] Relating this assertion to the encounter of the apostles with Jesus, he shows the change that occurred in their lives thus:

> Now they were new men in a new world, confident, courageous, enterprising, the leaders of a movement which made an immediate impact and went forward with an astonishing impetus. . . . It made them new men, but it was also the birth of a new community. . . . They themselves had passed through death to new life.[239]

Pink quoted by Benson O. Igboin gives further observable change that occurs in an individual's life when conversion takes place: "Salvation is a supernatural thing that changes the heart, renews the will, and transforms the life, so that it is evident to all around that a miracle of grade has been wrought."[240] ". . . a transparent moral character is to be noticed by the public in respect of the born-again's social life."[241] Therefore, this change "involves a

---

234. Orji, *Ethnic and Religious Conflicts*, 55.
235. Orji, 56.
236. Dunne, "Authentic Feminist Doctrine," 123.
237. Conn in Orji, *Ethnic and Religious Conflicts*, 56.
238. Dodd, *Founder of Christianity*, 37.
239. Dodd, 170–171.
240. Igboin, "Bias and Conversion," 178.
241. Dzurgba, *God and Caesar*, 54.

display of a high moral standard different from the pre-conversion experience. The gift of the Holy Spirit must be manifestly portrayed."[242] This change must be reflected in "their perception of realities, ideas, speech, taste, emotion or feeling, and action."[243] This change

> focuses on a thoroughgoing change from within one's mind and heart, so that one's way of relating to others is completely changed, starting from an entirely new space each day. It is not simply a shift to a new structural situation, but a way of living that opens to relocation and continuing change as one moves along the journey of life.[244]

Very profound observable changes occur, which demonstrate that an inward change has taken place. For instance, "believers undergo a radical change of lifestyle; they share their property, share their meals, and give careful attention to marginalized people (Acts 2:43–45; 4:32–33)."[245] These changed individuals "have to be constantly, relentlessly turning their ways of thinking, their education and training, their ways of working and doing things, toward Christ; they must think Christ into the patterns of thought they have inherited, into their networks of relationship and their processes for making decisions."[246]

A further observable change in the life of a convert is their engagement in sharing the Christian faith with other unbelieving persons. "The person who has been evangelized goes on to evangelize others. Here lies the test of truth, the touchstone of evangelization: it is unthinkable that a person should accept the Word and give himself to the kingdom without out becoming a person who bears witness to it and proclaims it in his turn."[247] For Christians, conversion is a change of heart and lifestyle which is reflected in the intellectual, religious, moral and affective life of the individual.

---

242. Igboin, "Bias and Conversion," 178.
243. Dzurgba, *God and Caesar*, 54.
244. Motte, "Conversion: A Missiological Perspective," 453.
245. Walls, "Converts or Proselytes?," 4.
246. Walls, 6.
247. Pope Paul VI, "Evangelii Nuntiandi," point 24.

Denominational Perspectives of Conversion

In various Christian traditions, conversion is viewed differently (i.e. it is understood differently between denominations). There are two different usages of conversion in Christian circles:

> In one stream conversion is spoken of essentially as an external act of religious change. In this usage Christian conversion refers to movement to the Christian faith, individually or collectively, on the part of people previously outside it. By extension, this usage can also indicate movement from one branch of Christian profession to another – from Catholic to Protestant, for instance, or vice versa.
>
> In the second usage, "conversion" denotes critical internal religious change in persons within the Christian community . . . Sometimes "conversion" refers to a subjective experience, sometimes to an assumed ontological change, sometimes to both.[248]

Evangelicals

This Christian tradition includes the charismatics and fundamentalists also because they share the same understanding of conversion with the evangelicals, though differ in certain theological positions and practices. Evangelicals perceive conversion to be a personal decision to follow Christ "effected by simple belief and prayer" through "believing certain doctrines, trusting Jesus for forgiveness, and praying a prayer of commitment."[249] This decision must be dramatic, more like Paul's experience on the road of Damascus; "it is sudden, it is a punctiliar event, and it is triggered by an encounter of some sort (with truth, with Jesus, with conviction of sin, and with the plan of salvation, etc.) that marks the beginning point of the Christian life."[250] This understanding of conversion has resulted in innumerable individuals who have made personal decisions to following Christ.

---

248. Walls, "Converts or Proselytes?," 2.
249. Peace, "Conflicting Understandings," 8.
250. Peace, 8.

Richard V. Peace points out three weaknesses or challenges with this kind of understanding of conversion. First, he argues that conversion is not "automatic or certain as evangelicals teach or imply. Biblically, the real challenge for the church is to make disciples (i.e., those who are actively and consciously following the way of Jesus), not to make converts (those who take a tentative first step toward Jesus)."[251] Second, this leaves the potential convert frustrated as they discover that they are unable to continue in Christian living. Once converts are won through crusades or evangelism, there is little contact with them for spiritual building, thereby abandoning them to survive on their own. Some of them fall away by the roadside. Lastly, this "perspective often fails to recognize that genuine conversion takes place in a variety of ways. . . . Most conversions take place over time, often with many fits and starts as one moves toward Jesus and his way."[252] As Peace has pointed out these weaknesses, in this kind of conversion, they may be considered an initial phase, it

> Must be taken as an initial one, yet sufficient to make a man realize that he has been snatched away from sin and led into the mystery of God's love, who called him to enter into a personal relationship with Him in Christ. For, by the workings of divine grace, the new convert sets out on a spiritual journey, by means of which, already sharing through faith in the mystery of Christ's Death and Resurrection, he passes from the old man to the new one, perfected in Christ (cf. Col. 3:5–10; Eph. 4:20–24).[253]

Pentecostals

Pentecostal understanding of conversion is similar to that of the evangelicals but differs in fervency of reaching out to sinners with the gospel of Christ.

> The Pentecostal view leads to a greater fervor in seeking to lead others to conversion . . . Pentecostal groups tend to practice continuous outreach involving every member. This evangelistic fervor comes from an eschatological urgency that insists that

---

251. Peace, 9.
252. Peace, 9.
253. Tynan, "New Evangelization," 48.

> time is short – the Lord may return, or you may die – so decide for Jesus today![254]

Additionally, Pentecostal conversions "are typically more intense than those experienced by evangelicals because it is often accompanied by signs of power that convince converts that God is immediately active and present in their lives."[255] They are fervent in their primary goal, which is to bring people to Christ, getting people saved, and getting them born again. These are all phrases or concepts of conversion which "mean the process of bringing people who are not presently Christian (or those who have not had a definitive experience of coming into relationship with Jesus) into a lived experience of relationship and communication with Jesus Christ."[256]

Mainline Protestants

For this group,

> Christianity is a matter more of nurture than of decision; the key decision is made on behalf of individuals as parents bring their infant children for baptism. The decision later required of these baptized children when they become adults has more to do with continuing alignment with the community than with following Jesus. The key activities of post baptism nurture in mainline churches are Sunday School instruction (for children), catechism and confirmation (for teens), and active participation in church leadership (for adults).[257]

Peace posits that the mainline church today "no longer holds a single view of conversion, nor is the operative view of conversion based on Reformation theology. Rather, it emerges from whatever central image captivates a particular congregation or denomination."[258] The challenge with this position, Peace argues, is that "conversion and the work of conversion (i.e. evangelism) drift from the center of one's ecclesiastical vision;"[259] faith for the mainline church

---

254. Peace, "Conflicting Understandings," 9.
255. Peace, 9.
256. Tynan, "New Evangelization," 47.
257. Peace, "Conflicting Understandings," 9.
258. Peace, 9.
259. Peace, 9.

becomes extrinsic (nominalism), not intrinsic (inner conviction) and there is an absence of teaching what it means to be a child of God. "This perspective calls people to community without sufficient focus on what it means to be a child of God, whose primary allegiance is to Jesus. Faith in Jesus needs to be internalized in order to be real."[260]

He ends by suggesting that,

> Mainline churches need to help their membership commit themselves consciously to what is implicit in church activity and membership. Without such consciousness, church membership makes little difference in your life and the lives of others. We need to create ways for people to grow in all aspects of faith: belief, commitment, service, relationships, justice, spirituality, and more.[261]

Catholics

The Catholic understanding of conversion is centered on "the reality of the church and its sacraments."[262] Conversion in Catholicism implies "entering into an ecclesial reality that embraces, at once, a historical institution and the Mystical Body – one which claims to contain all the redemptive activity of God in history."[263]

> Sacraments are administered not only as the means of grace but as instruments of unity in the church. The sacraments place the whole of the conversion process in its communal and historical context. What may begin for a person in the study of old books, with a passionate concern for injustice, or in the crucible of personal guilt must be opened to the presence and radical dependence upon the whole body of other baptized Christians – past, present, and future.[264]

---

260. Peace, 10.
261. Peace, 9–10.
262. Hudson, "Catholic View of Conversion," 117.
263. Hudson, 118.
264. Hudson, 118.

Some of these sacraments, for instance, the sacrament of baptism "represent the turning point of conversion, particularly for adults. Baptism confers the grace of justification in the remission of sin and is the beginning of the process of inward sanctification."[265] The sacrament of confirmation "continues what baptism began. By the laying on of hands, the baptized person is given the sanctifying grace for growth in beatitude."[266] The importance of baptism in conversion is further buttressed by some Popes, such as Pope Eugene IV:

> Holy baptism, which is the gateway to the spiritual life, holds the first place among all the sacraments; through it we are made members of Christ and of the body of the Church. And since death entered the universe through the first man, "unless we are born again of water and the Spirit, we cannot," as the Truth says, "enter into the kingdom of heaven" (John 3:5). The matter of this sacrament is real and natural water.[267]

Also shown by Pope Innocent III, "But the sacrament of baptism is consecrated in water at the invocation of the undivided Trinity – namely, Father, Son, and Holy Ghost – and brings salvation to both children and adults when it is correctly carried out by anyone in the form laid down by the church."[268]

Pope Pius XI said, "Indeed this kingdom is presented in the Gospels as such, into which men prepare to enter by doing penance; moreover, they cannot enter it except through faith and baptism, which, although an external rite, yet signifies and affects an interior regeneration."[269] Since there is no salvation outside of the "historical institution and the Mystical body" and "since there is no entering into the Catholic Church of Christ without the Sacrament of Baptism, this means that only baptized Catholics who die in the state of grace (and those who become baptized Catholics and die in the state of grace) can hope to be saved – *period*."[270] Though conversion is more sacramental

---

265. Hudson, 118.

266. Hudson, 118.

267. Pope Eugene IV, *The Council of Florence*, "Exultate Deo," November 22, 1439 quoted in Battad, "Sacrament of Baptism."

268. Pope Innocent III, *Fourth Lateran Council*, Constitution 1, 1215, *ex cathedra* quote in Battad, "Sacrament of Baptism."

269. Pope Pius XI, *Quas Primas* (no. 15), December 11, 1925 quoted in Battad, "Sacrament of Baptism."

270. Dimond, *Outside the Catholic Church*, 6.

for the Catholics, there are some who believe that conversion to Christ is much deeper than just the sacrament. "In Catholic tradition there are many examples of the experience of conversion to Jesus Christ being lived with an overwhelming affective/psychological component."[271] According to Pope Paul VI, this conversion is "a total interior renewal which the Gospel calls metanoia; it is a radical conversion, a profound change of mind and heart."[272] For the purpose of this discussion on Catholic understanding of conversion, I follow the popular notion of conversion of the Catholic being sacramental.

Orthodox

The Orthodox Church's perspective of conversion is somewhat similar to that of the Roman Catholic's in its strong emphasis on liturgy, priests, community and, perhaps, sacrament and ecclesial emphases.

> The Church holds that the good news of Jesus Christ must be proclaimed to all men, and if some of the audience have not heard it to conviction or have received it in a limited or defective state, no effort may be spared to bring them to a full understanding so that they may be baptized into the Christian fellowship which is the Body of Christ, the Kingdom of God on earth, the Orthodox Church. . . . By the supernatural effects of the visible, material washing with water and anointing with *Myron* all sins are forgiven and a new creature emerges from the fount. This is a community sacrament, a mystery of the whole body, and apart from or outside of the Church it is empty and meaningless. . . . The communal quality of the Mystery of Baptism is illustrated by the numerous accounts of the baptism of whole tribes and peoples at one time in the more active missionary campaigns of the Church and by the common practice of infant baptism, in which priest, sponsor, and congregation achieve potentially the salvation of a soul incapable of acting on its own behalf and still largely unaware of the world around it.[273]

---

271. Tynan, "New Evangelization," 49.
272. Pope Paul VI, "Evangelii Nuntiandi."
273. Schneirla, "Conversion in the Orthodox Church," 91.

Membership in the Orthodox Church is in infancy through baptism, "The Church will provide instruction in due time and appropriate measure and will expect individual response in faith, but a saving conversion has been, as it were, imposed by the community of Christ, the Church."[274]

Membership into the church by non-Orthodox background individuals is also allowed, but certain requirement must be adhered to.

> Adults wishing to join the Orthodox Church are encouraged to attend an Orthodox Church so as to become familiar with the services and how to take part in them. Then, in due course, they are baptized and undergo chrismation, a sacrament similar to confirmation. Once baptized, such a person is a member of God's family, which is the key issue.[275]

From the Orthodox perspective, salvation is obtained in the church: "No one is saved alone. He who is saved is saved in the Church, as a member of and in union with all her other members."[276] Thus, salvation is sacramental and ecclesial. Peace posits that "the word 'conversion' does not seem to be part of the functional vocabulary in the Orthodox Church. It is not that Orthodoxy is uninterested in conversion, salvation, justification, or sanctification but that it talks about these realities in a different way."[277]

As has observed in the above various denominations understanding of conversion, conversion is multifaceted, complex, and dynamic. No single position encapsulates the nature of conversion. Peace was able to incorporate all these various perspectives of conversion in a sentence which brings vividly the full nature of Christian conversion:

> The real question when it comes to Christian conversion is conscious commitment to Jesus (by repentance and faith). Such a commitment is expressed in a variety of ways – through belief, via baptism and confirmation, in membership and participation in a Christian community, through participation in the sacraments. In the end, *conversion is about the human experience of*

---

274. Schneirla, 91.
275. Peace, "Conflicting Understandings," 10.
276. Ware, *Orthodox Way*, 133.
277. Peace, "Conflicting Understandings," 10.

God's saving grace – awareness, consciousness, commitment, deliberately turning one's life around, coming to a whole new understanding of what life is all about.[278]

I have established that Christian conversion is asking Jesus for forgiveness of sins, trusting him alone for external life, turning from sins, and following him through a simple prayer of faith. I also established that when a person becomes a Christian there are observable changes that occur in their life in the area of intellect, religion, moral and affective, and others. Finally, I showed different perspectives of conversion in various Christian traditions. In the preceding section, I shall discuss the Muslim understanding of conversion.

Islamic Understanding of Conversion

There appears to be no general Arabic word for the concept of conversion in Islamic thought "but there is a verb *aslama* that conveys the idea of becoming a Muslim and literally means to submit."[279] This submission toward Allah is demonstrated by believing in the Oneness of Allah, be devoted to him, obeying his stipulations, and forsaking what he has prohibited. So, "what non-Muslims would call 'conversion to the Muslim faith' Muslims describe by such words as *islam* (surrender to God), *imam* (faith in God), and *ihtida* (following the right guidance). Conversely, what non-Muslims would call 'conversion from the Muslim faith' Muslims call *irtidad* (apostasy)."[280] Nieuwkerk's research among new Muslims in the West validates this notion but the new Muslims prefer using terms like "to become a Muslim," "to take Shahada," "reversion," "to accept Islam," or "to embrace Islam," to describe their conversion to Islam.[281]

She provides three reasons for this variation; first, the concept of conversion is perceived as an etic perspective while reverting to Islam is considered an emic view. Second, conversion connotes a "radical change, a change to something new."[282] Some of her interviewees felt they were not changing to

---

278. Peace, 12.
279. Nieuwkerk, "'Islam Is Your Birthright,'" 155.
280. Woodberry, "Conversion in Islam," 22.
281. Nieuwkerk, "'Islam Is Your Birthright,'" 154–155.
282. Nieuwkerk, 155.

something new because "they already felt Muslim but did not know that their ideas ... were Islamic."[283] Lastly, Islam claims that everyone is born a Muslim, but the family the child was born into brought the child up in a different religion. When people embrace Islam, they are simply returning to their original religion. Her point on conversion connoting a radical change and using it to validate the Islamic concept of conversion seems narrow because conversion also connotes gradual change, change of affiliation, adhesion, acculturation, transformation, breaking away from the old and turning to the new, and / or change of orthodoxy to intensification. I think researchers interested in conversion studies need to understand these various connotations in order to understand people's testimonies of conversion. Her third point (reversion) I consider an important factor, because it explains the ideology of conversion in Islam.

Having discovered various terms used in conveying the concept of conversion in Islam, what then is conversion? According to Murad "Coming to Islam is like going back to one's own roots in nature, and in history."[284] Reversion "means the return to a pure, sinless state of submission to God. People go back to a natural and inborn disposition to follow God."[285] This definition is clearly elaborated and explained vividly by the writer of The Modern Religion website, who emphatically describes Islam as a birthright.

> Islam states clearly that everyone is born a Muslim and is therefore monotheistic by nature. We read in the Qur'an that humanity has been created with the natural disposition towards the unity of God. This is to be expected, for Allah, who has breathed His spirit into each of us, is Himself the example of perfect unity. In the words of the Prophet Muhammad: "Every person is born with the innate religious faith (to submit to God Almighty)." Thus when an individual accepts Islam, he is not turning his back on any prior revelation but rather is returning to the original and true revelation of Allah and to his own nature as a creation of Allah. This being the case, Islam is your

---

283. Nieuwkerk, 155.
284. Murad, *Da'wah among Non-Muslims*, 16.
285. Murad, 161.

birthright-other religious or ideological systems are either corruptions or outright denials of Islam.[286]

When non-Muslims embrace Islam, they are not converting to a new religion or changing allegiance to another, but returning to the original religion chosen and perfected for them. "This day I have perfected your religion for you, completed My favor upon you, and have chosen for you Islam as your religion" (5:3). Muhammad says in the hadith, "No child is born but upon *fitra*. It is his parents who make him a Jew or a Christian or a Polytheist."[287] Conversion to Islam is simply returning to the original state of sinless and to the old original and natural religion "chosen" and "perfected" by Allah. Murad portrays this point succinctly:

> We do not invite people to a "new" religion, we invite them to the oldest religion, indeed to their "own" religion, the religion of living in total surrender to their Creator, in accordance with the guidance brought by all His Messengers. Indeed, if I am not misunderstood, we may be bold enough to say that we do not invite anyone to change his "religion", to transfer his allegiance to a rival religion. For, by our own admission, Islam is not a new or rival religion among the many competing for human allegiance; it is the natural and primordial religion. All nature lives in submission to its Creator; all Messengers – Adam to Muhammad – brought the same religion.[288]

By this assertion, Islam pre-dates other religions, contradicts historical facts. Murad appears to be giving excessive credit to Islam and neglecting historical fact.

> Moreover, by ascribing to itself the status of *din al-fitra*, Islam puts itself outside the fold of history and historical scrutiny, while other religions are seen as nothing but historical developments, perceived as deviations from the *din al-fitra*, Islam. Such an approach stigmatizes other religions and their adherents and thus precludes possibility of any fruitful dialogue between

---

286. "Islam Is Your Birthright," Islamway.net, https://en.islamway.net/article/8259.
287. Sahih Muslim, 195, II, 8:53.
288. Murad, *Da'wah among Non-Muslims*, 18.

Muslims and non-Muslims, even if the latter were willing to engage in one.[289]

Given a cursory look at both religious faiths, Christianity and Islam, one may conclude that both are similar, therefore there is no difference. Lamin Sanneh provides some distinct similarity between both religions thus:

> The picture of mission and renewal in Christian Africa has some interesting parallels with Muslim Africa. To find a good example we have to turn to African Christian Independency and the prophet movements it spawned. We see, for instance, an identical religious commitment expressing itself in the call to repentance and to change in lifestyle, the same resolve to make Scripture the rule of religious activity in personal and public life, and the same wish to recapture for Africa the original promises of God. In both cases we find close attention to details of ritual purity, to matters of sartorial propriety. There is the same regard for public character of religion, for the display in public places of appropriate religious symbolism and imagery. Reform Islam sought to rivet the code on the lukewarm and fainthearted, while prophet movements aspired to a similar commitment among their followers. In each case the "Word of God" was understood to carry great power, and therefore those religious leaders who had access to it were believed to possess commensurate authority and influence.[290]

Theologically, conversion in Islam entails acceptance of the oneness of Allah – that there is no other god but Allah; he has neither partners nor son. This is because Islam believes that other religions like Christianity are polytheistic in nature. Converts from Christianity to Islam reject the Trinity and the Sonship of Christ Jesus, which Islam perceives as associating partners to Allah. Converts are also returning to a sinless nature of man since Allah created man sinless, so there is no need for transformation from original sin as Christians believe.

---

289. Racius, "Multiple Nature," 96.
290. Sanneh, *Translating the Message*, 271.

As I look at the Igbo converts to Islam, I now understand what they convert to. Many of them claim that Christians and Muslims worship the same God, but theologically, they are not. Muslims deny the divinity of Christ, the Trinity, and Jesus Christ as the only way to God. When an Igbo Christian reverts to Islam they reject this Christian doctrine and returns to the Islamic belief of the oneness of Allah. This Allah is significantly different from the Christian God, about whom Christians teach as one God, but three in essence. People's change to Islam is at various levels: "first was 'total conversion' by those who inwardly accepted its spirit and principles. The second was 'formal adhesion' by those who accepted the outward duties, but did not accept in their spirits. The third was 'enforced adherence' by those who are kept in the alliance by force or threat of force."[291] These various levels of commitment to Islam are also observed in present day conversions to Islam.

> I observed a great variety of patterns, commitments and changes. Some radically changed many aspects of their identities, convictions and lifestyles, whereas others gradually changed their lifestyles but, for instance, did not alter their names or outward appearance. Some changed abruptly, and then gradually relaxed their religious commitment, while others slowly built up their religious commitment. Yet in the end most of them substantially changed their lifestyles and world views.[292]

These various levels of conversion confirm the uniqueness and multifaceted nature of conversion.

Biblical Understanding of Conversion

This section discusses the root words and meaning of biblical conversion specifically from the Old and New Testaments (OT and NT), as well as the nature of Christian conversion. In addition, theological implications are also explained. "To convert is derived from the original Hebrew, Greek, and Latin

---

291. Woodberry, "Conversion in Islam," 25.
292. Nieuwkerk, "'Islam Is Your Birthright,'" 157.

terms meaning to turn, to return, and to turn again (as well as turning, returning, and turning about)."[293] Let us discuss this in detail.

Old Testament Conversion

The term conversion is derived from the Hebrew word *sub* which means,

> turning away from someone (Jer. 32:40); turning back to God; turning to follow someone (Ruth 1:15); stop proceeding with an action (Jug 11:35); to turn from evil (Mal. 2:6); repent of sin (1 Kg 3:35); or return to a master or mistress, submit oneself to him or her, obey his or her orders, give allegiance to a king (1 Kgs 12:27; Gen. 16:9; Jg. 11:8; 1 Kg 12:27).[294]

It could also mean "to turn around, repent, and to be changed."[295] An important meaning of *sub* is "to turn back to God (Yahweh); be devoted to God (Yahweh)."[296] Victor P. Hamilton supports Ludwig Koehler and Walter Baumgartner by further identifying a specific nation required to turn back to God. He asserts that "the theological aspect and most crucial meaning of *sub* is in passages dealing with the covenant community's return to God (in the sense of repentance), or turning away from evil (in the sense of renouncing and disowning sin), or turning away from God (in the sense of becoming apostate)"[297] Christoph Barth provided an all-inclusive meaning of *sub* as a "turning in the opposite direction. The direction in which a person went or looked and which determined his plans and actions are changed anew, in the opposite direction. It means a re-orientation towards a goal from which one has moved away previously."[298]

The words "turn away" and "return" are comprehensive and inclusive. It was a call to the Israelites (1 Kgs 8:35) to the Nenevites (Jonah 3:10), to people (Jer 15:7), to nation(s) (Jer 18:33), to man (Jer 18:11; 23:14; Jonah 3:8), to the house of Israel (Ezek 33:11), to wicked one (Ezek 3:19), and to everyone. It is also explicit in what to turn away from, such as transgression

---

293. Paloutzian, Richardson, and Rambo, "Religious Conversion," 1051.
294. Clines, *Dictionary of Classical Hebrew*, 278.
295. Koehler and Baumgartner, *Hebrew and Aramaic Lexicon*, 1427–1428.
296. Koehler and Baumgartner, 1429.
297. Hamilton, s.v. "Shub," 909.
298. Barth, "Notes on 'return' in the Old Testament," 310.

(Ezek 18:28), iniquity (Job 36:10; Dan 9:13), evil (Jer 25:5), wickedness (Ezek 18:27; 33:12), violence (Jonah 3:8), an evil deed (Zech 1:4; Neh. 9:35), or an evil way (1 Kgs 13:33; 17:13).

In the prophetic books, *sub* is frequently "associated with the challenge to the covenant community of Israel to return to God from their false worship. It is especially important to note that the context of this prophetic theme is in regards to the covenant community of Israel, who needed to return to her God."[299] Edmond Jacob explained this specific context vividly asserting that,

> to "turn" means Israel's return to its origins, that is, the pure and unalloyed covenant with Yahweh. . . . This return necessarily implies a breaking of relationship: to return to Yahweh must bring the forsaking of foreign gods (Hosea 2:9) and certain cultic and cultural forms incompatible with Yahweh: political alliance and trust in military force are just as much signs of unfaithfulness because they are a challenge to Yahweh's sovereignty.[300]

Barth concurs with Jacob that turn means the return of Israel to God, whom they had forsaken. He likened the Israelites' return to an unfaithful wife returning to her rightful Lord and spouse. However he went further, asserting that *sub* also "means turning away from the false, illegal, alien 'lords,' and from the world dominated by them."[301]

Samuel Waje Kunhiyop's understanding of *sub* is noteworthy because he included an ethical dimension to the meaning of *sub*, which appears absent in other meanings of *sub* examined. According to him, "Sub and other idioms indicate that conversion is a turning which involves a change of direction. The sinner turns away from sin to faith in the God of Israel. The Old Testament demonstrates that this change also involves a change in moral and ethical behavior."[302] He demonstrated his point with the stories of Naaman, Josiah, and the Ninevites.

Sub was primarily associated with the Israelites being urged to return from their false worship to the true God. This understanding, as already mentioned above, is clearly bolstered in the prophetic literature: "The perverse

---

299. Kunhiyop, *Christian Conversion in Africa*, 14.
300. Jacob, *Theology of the Old Testament*, 289.
301. Barth, "Notes on 'return' in the Old Testament," 310.
302. Kunhiyop, *Christian Conversion in Africa*, 14.

Israelites were confronted by the eloquence of Isaiah, Jeremiah, Ezekiel, and others who urged them to forsake their idolatry and immorality, and to turn toward the merciful God who created them, provided for them, and led them out of bondage into the new life of the Promised Land."[303] For example: "Let the wicked forsake their ways, and the unrighteous their thoughts; let them return to the Lord, and he will have mercy on them, and to our God, for he will freely pardon." (Isa 55:7; cf. Ezek 18–30, 32; Hos 14:2).

Based on the above explanation of *sub*, I would rearticulate biblical conversion in the OT to mean: to turn back or repent from sin, evil, and wickedness, coupled with a return to God; to desist from previous actions, no longer proceed with evil actions, and follow God; return to God and submit to his orders, obey him, and give him allegiance. It means a change of one's mind. Brown rightly summarized this when he asserts that "conversion is described in the Old Testament as turning from evil (Jer 18:8) to the Lord (Mal. 3:7)."[304] An obvious observation from the meaning of *sub* is that it shows who to turn to or return to (God) and what to turn away from (sin, wickedness, evil, etc.). Conversion "involves a complete change from one life-style to another. It may require abandoning an aimless and unsatisfying perspective in exchange for a new and promising incentive to live a more meaningful life."[305]

Having established the OT root word and meaning of conversion, the following section shows that the NT shares a similar meaning, but conversion was more particularly an individual event as opposed to a community event as seen in the OT, as along with added faith and repentance.

New Testament Conversion

In the New Testament, "there are three related word groups that express the concept of conversion: *epistrepho, metanoeo,* and *metamelomai.*"[306] *Epistrepho:* according to F. Laubach,

> is found 36 times in the NT, and in addition in variant readings in Lk. 10:6, Acts 15:16, 2 Pet. 2:21, 18 times it has its secular meaning of turning, returning, turning away, etc. (cf. Matt.

---

303. Kerr and Mulder, *Famous Conversions*, ix.
304. Brown, *New International Dictionary*, 354.
305. Kerr and Mulder, *Famous Conversions*, ix.
306. Peace, *Conversion in the New Testament*, 346.

10:13; 2 Pet. 2:22), and 18 times with its theological meaning of conversion, especially in Acts and the Epistles (cf. Mk. 4:12; Lk. 1:16f; 22:32; Acts 15:19; 2 Cor. 3:16; Jas. 5:19f.[307]

In his attempt to explain how this word is used in the New Testament he writes,

> When men are called in the NT to conversion, it means a fundamentally new turning of the human will to God, a return home from blindness and error to the Saviour of all (Acts 26:18; 1 Pet. 2:25). The use of *epistrepho* suggests that we are not concerned primarily with turning from the old life, but the stress is on the turning to Christ, and through him to God (cf. Jn. 14:1, 6) and so to a new life.[308]

Peace shows that *epistrepho* has similarity with *sub* used in the Old Testament for conversion. He additionally brings out more actions or attitude one turns away from, which when combined with Laubach's, gives a richer understanding of *epistrepho*. The use of *epistrepho* in the New Testament bears a lot of similarity to the way *sub* is used in the Old Testament.

> The turning is from wicked ways (Acts 3:26), from the error of one's ways (James 5:20), from darkness to light and from power of Satan to God (Acts 26:18), from worthless things to the living God (Acts 14:15), from idols to serve the living and true God (1 Thess. 1:9), from going astray to the Shepherd and Overseer of one's soul (1 Pet. 2:25); the turning is to the Lord (Acts 9:35; 11:21;15:19;26:20;2 Cor.3:16); the result of turning is forgiveness of sin and times of refreshment (Acts 3:19;26:18).[309]

Metanoeo means "change of one's mind, repent, be converted."[310] J. Goetzmann asserts that "*metanoeo* is equivalent to the Heb. *Niham*, to be sorry about something. It is used of God in 1 Sam. 15:29. Hence if the change of mind involves the recognition that the previous opinion was false or bad, we get the meaning to feel remorse or regret."[311] *Metanoeo* is used distinctively

---

307. Laubach, "Epistrepho," 355.
308. Laubach, 355.
309. Peace, *Conversion in the New Testament*, 348.
310. Goetzman, "Metanoia," 358.
311. Laubach, "Epistrepho," 355.

in the New Testament to "discern first and foremost the preaching of John the Baptist in the light of the Qumran movement."[312] Goetzmann says,

> The closest link with the prophetic call to repentance is undoubtedly found in John the Baptist, who called the people to repentance and to "bear fruit that befits repentance" (Matt. 3:2). Corresponding to the OT pattern, the call was addressed to the whole people (cf. Acts 13:24; 19:4) and also to the pious, who believed that they did not need to repent (Matt. 3:7ff.) John, like the rest of the NT, based the urgency of his message on a different foundation from that of the prophets. Motivation in the OT for repentance and returning along the true road of God's righteousness was linked with the past and its social unrighteousness and idolatry. For John it was that "the kingdom of heaven is at hand" (Matt. 3:2). Hence, there can be only one way for the man wishing to escape judgment. He must repent, so that his whole life is changed and brought into a new relationship with God (Matt. 3:10).[313]

Metanoeo conveys that repentance is very vital in the conversion experience of a man. Kunhiyop helps us understand this by identifying four important metaphors that illustrate the meaning of conversion in the NT: repentance, faith, baptism, and rich.[314] According to Kunhiyop, "repentance was an important subject of the disciples' preaching (Mk. 6:12; Acts 26:20). Failure to repent leads to destruction (Lk. 13:3,5; Mtt. 11:20). God also commands all men everywhere to repent (Acts 17:30, 2:38, 3:19, 5:31, 18:22, 20:21)."[315]

The importance of repentance in conversion in the NT is further explained by W. G. Kummel,

> *Metanoia* (repentance) is an essential pre-condition for withstanding the judgment of God or for entering into God's Kingdom (Mt. 11:21–22, 12:14). This call for *metanoia* is central both in the message of the prophets and also in later Judaism. Its

---

312. Peace, *Conversion in the New Testament*, 350.
313. Goetzmann, "Metanoia," 358.
314. Kunhiyop, *Christian Conversion in Africa*, 28.
315. Kunhiyop, 29.

> main object is not in the first place to awaken a feeling of guilt, although this is naturally not excluded (Mt.11:21; Lk. 7:37–38). Its primary content is the demand that man should turn aside from the wrong way and embark upon the way which is the will of God (cf. especially the parable of the Prodigal Son: (Lk. 15:11–12, and also Lk. 9:62).[316]

Repentance, therefore, "is now no longer obedience to a law but to a person. The call to repentance becomes a call to discipleship. So repentance, faith and discipleship are different aspects of the same thing (Mk. 1:15, 'Repent and believe')."[317] Just like repentance, faith is another vital aspect of conversion in the NT. Peace elaborates on this as he differentiates between repentance and faith:

> Repentance (*metanoia*) begins with the cognitive decision to turn. A choice is made. A decision is reached. The decision to turn, however, is not the turning itself. That which activates repentance and moves it from a mental decision to a behavioral activity is faith (*pistis*). When a person looks back and decides to leave behind (turn away from) certain errant ways or false gods, that is repentance. When that same person looks ahead in trust and confidence to Jesus as the one who can and will forgive, that is faith. Repentance and faith taken together result in conversion in the New Testament sense.[318]

Wallis provides further understanding of faith and repentance as they relate to conversion.

> As repentance is the turning from, faith is the turning to. Repentance is seeing our sin and turning from it, faith is seeing Jesus and turning toward him. Together, repentance and faith form the two movements of conversion. Faith is turning to belief, hope, and trust. As repentance dealt with our past, faith

---

316. Kummel, *Man in the New Testament*, 18–19.
317. Goetzmann, "Metanoia," 358.
318. Peace, *Conversion in the New Testament*, 352.

opens up our future. Faith opens us to the future by restoring our sight, softening our hearts, and bringing light into our darkness.[319]

Repentance and faith are indispensable elements of conversion and are closely linked in the NT. For conversion to occur, these two must be present. To wrap up our study of *metanoeo*,

> *Metanoeo*, then, is the key word symbolizing the character of the response on the part of men to the preaching of the judgment and the rule of God. It marks a total turning on God's terms, a movement from the direction in which they are going to its opposite in order to be re-established in a relationship of faithfulness to their covenant-God. It draws its force, in part from the past that is, from the prophets, and this serves as the bearer of the verb *shuv* (*shubh*) in its highest potency. But, it also draws its force, in part, from the present events marking the end-time. The new motif which gives a unique energy to the *metanoia* of the New Testament is the eschatological reality in face of the imminent rule of God.[320]

Metamelomai (change one's mind, regret, repent) is the last word cluster regarding conversion in the NT and is related to *metanoeo* because both involve regret and repentance. Though Laubach argues that *metamelomai* "cannot always be clearly distinguished from *metanoeo*, which implies that in retrospect one thinks differently about a matter."[321] Peace acknowledges that the terms are related:

> in that it involves regret over past actions – a change of mind about them. However, it differs from *metanoeo* in that *metamelomai* is more a feeling than a decision, much less an action. The sense of *metamelomai* is that one regrets a past deed but does not decide necessarily never to do it again, much less to express this new view in concrete action (e.g., restitution). *Metanoeo*

---

319. Jim Wallis, *Call to Conversion*, 5.
320. Heikkinen, "'Conversion,'" 5.
321. Laubach, "Epistrepho," 365.

is a stronger word and the one that bears upon the process of conversion.[322]

Laubach provides excellent biblical accounts that illustrate the difference between *metamelomai* and *metanoeo*:

> The example of Judas makes it clear that *metamelomai* and *metanoeo* do not have identical meanings in the NT. Judas recognized that Jesus had been wrongly condemned. He regretted his betrayal (Mt.27:3), but he did not find the way to genuine repentance. We find the same differentiation in 2 Cor. 7:8–10. Paul did not regret that he had written a sharp letter to the Corinthians, for the sorrow caused to its recipients had led them to true repentance (*metanoia*), to an inner turning to God. There is no need to regret such a repentance, for it always serves only our salvation.[323]

So metanoeo is more than human regret or remorse; it involves a deliberate decision to desist from the action regretted. There are several metaphors or figures of speech that illustrate conversion in the NT writings:

> It can be a transfer out of darkness into light (1 Pet. 2:9), a spiritual rebirth or being born again (Jn. 3:3), a restoration from impurity (Titus 2:14), a translation from death to life (Jn. 5:24), a turning away from Satan to God (Acts 26:18), a totally new creation (11 Cor. 5:17), a getting rid of an old and acquiring a new humanity (Co. 3:9), a dying to self but rising again in Christ (Rom. 6:2–8).[324]

Theologically, conversion has a varied theological meaning,

> The biblical words for "turn" can have a very broad range of theological meaning. In relation to God they can denote God's turning to His people, His turning from them, His turning of them, and even perhaps His preventing of their turning to Him. In relation to man the terms have similar range. People turn

---

322. Peace, *Conversion in the New Testament*, 351.
323. Laubach, "Epistrepho," 356.
324. Kerr and Mulder, *Famous Conversions*, ix.

from God, turn (back) to idols, turn (again) from idols, turn (back) to God, return to their land, turn from idols, turn (back) to God, return to their land, turn others to God, turn people to one another, turn back those who are in error, or even turn the gospel into its opposite.[325]

As we can see, the root word and meaning of conversion in the NT is turning from evil ways and returning to God in repentance and faith. As reviewed, both the OT and NT root words for conversion point to a turning and returning. Turning away from evil, wickedness and unrighteousness, and returning to God. The concept of conversion was initially associated in the OT with Israel's challenge to return from false worship to Yahweh, their God, but it is also a challenge in the NT to individuals, and everyone, to return to God by turning back from sin. Let us now consider the nature of conversion.

Paloutzian, Richardson, and Rambo capture the nature of conversion clearly, asserting that,

As used in the Bible, the words turn, return, and turn again refer to actions of movement and theological notions of a person or group's orientation to God, the community of faith, and moral action. In the Hebrew Bible, the term almost always refers to a person within the Jewish community who repents because he or she or a group violated fundamental principles of their covenant with God, either in moral or theological wrongdoings. In the New Testament, the term points to another reality: People outside the covenant of God are being included in the new community of faith. The Book of Acts, for instance, tells stories of Jews who accept Jesus as the Messiah and of Gentiles who embrace a new faith and a new way of life.[326]

Factors Influencing Religious Conversion

There are various factors influencing religious conversion. Gooren categorized these into five main groups: "individual factors, social factors, institutional

---

325. Bromiley, *International Standard Bible*, 768.
326. Paloutzian, Richardson, and Rambo, "Religious Conversion," 1051–1052.

factors (related to the religious organization), cultural factors (including political and economic factors), and contingency factors. Contingency factors involve random meetings with missionaries, acutely felt crises, and other contingencies that bring individuals into the realm of religious groups."[327]

Gooren highlights how according to Manuela Cantón Delgado's actor-oriented model,

> the main reasons for conversion are personal: a dissatisfaction with Catholicism, feelings of crisis and great personal suffering (economic, social, and family problems, often connected to alcoholism), and a need for spirituality and personal control. A special event – a serious illness, a fierce hangover – serves as a catalyst for conversion, which always constitutes a radical transformation in the believer's perspective.[328]

Ikenga-Metuh posits four major factors responsible for conversion to Christianity and to Islam from the primal religion in Africa; "the shattered microcosm, the intellectualist theory, an historical explanation, and a social-structural explanation."[329] He argues that Christianity and Islam were successful in Africa because they coincided with periods of social and cultural change: modernization, colonialism, and industrialization. Also an increased number of mushrooming indigenous movements contributed to rapid conversions in Africa. He further asserts, "It is not only the response of traditional tribal cultures to modernization, but also a response of Africans and African Religions to Islam and missionary Christianity."[330] Ikenga-Metuh's position enables researchers like me to be broad in our search for reasons for conversion from one religion to another. It also sounds a warning to scholars of conversion studies that no single factor is sufficient to explain the conversion phenomenon. Therefore, we must look out for as many factors as possible to enable us to understand the conversion phenomenon in the world today. Though Ikenga-Metuh focused on conversion from primal religion to Christianity and Islam, the factors he identified may explain conversion from Christianity to Islam and vice versa, that this work seeks to understand.

---

327. Gooren, "Anthropology of Religious Conversion," 100.
328. Gooren, 98.
329. Ikenga-Metuh, "Shattered Microcosm," 11–12.
330. Ikenga-Metuh, 12.

Ottenberg discovered in his research among the Afikpo people of Igboland that descent and kin ties were key factors involved in their conversion to Islam.[331] Ikenga-Metuh pointed out a similar factor and others, including: "inter-marriage, family and kinship ties; social prestige; patron-client relationships; and a desire not to be labeled as a 'pagan' or 'primitive,' as Christian and Muslim missionary propaganda called adherents of traditional religion."[332]

Dissatisfaction with one's present situation, previous religion, social tension, feelings of meaninglessness, unresolved crisis, and the like, can also influence conversion.[333] Some individuals convert to a new religion based on the opportunity it provides for mobility; the case of Ewe people of Ghana depicts this.[334] Other factors include economic mobility, intellectualist factors, unresolved tension and crises from childhood to adulthood, disappointment and failure, desire to know God better, and sense of love and acceptance. To explain people's conversion motives, there is first the need to consider the factors and theories of conversion.

Conclusion

In this chapter, I briefly discussed the history of the Igbo, noting that they are located in the eastern part of Nigeria. The Igbo area is the most populous Christian region in Nigeria. In fact, it is known as the "Heartland of Christianity in Nigeria."[335] The Igbo were originally traditional worshipers, then converted to Christianity via the early missionaries. From the middle years of the last century, Christianity was established in Igboland. This is how they came to predominantly follow the Christian religion in Nigeria.

I also explored various definitions of religious conversion, including an interdisciplinary perspective between anthropology and psychology. Though religious conversion is complex, many scholars agree that it is primarily a gradual process rather than a sudden one. In Christendom, religious conversion involves accepting Jesus Christ as personal Lord and Savior by means of

---

331. Ottenberg, "Moslem Igbo Village," 240.
332. Ikenga-Metuh, "Shattered Microcosm," 23.
333. Gerlach and Hine, *People, Power, Change*, 110.
334. Meyer, *Translating the Devil*, 11.
335. Ozigboh, *History of Igboland*, 5

a simple prayer of repentance and faith. Meanwhile Islam perceives religious conversion as reversion; a return to the natural and inborn disposition to follow God. As a Christian, writing from a Christian viewpoint, conversion is more than returning to a natural disposition to follow God because the natural and inborn disposition of man is sinful. Rather it is more of a returning to God, through Jesus Christ, for the forgiveness and cleansing of sin, including the Adamic sin. This is state obtained by faith in Jesus Christ through repentance.

CHAPTER 3

Research Methodology

The purpose of this study was to identify the reasons the Igbo Christians give for their conversion to Islam. This chapter discusses the research methodology: review of the appropriateness of the research methods design, as well as a brief discussion of sample and population. In addition, data collection procedure, data analysis procedure and validation are also discussed.

Research Design

For this study, the qualitative research method was adopted. The philosophical assumption behind this research method claims that "meanings are constructed by human beings as they engage with the world they are interpreting."[1] In other words, the inquirer seeks to understand a reality that is assumed by a specified group of subjects, unlike the post-positivists where a researcher first adopts existing hypotheses and then proceeds to test its validity. In qualitative research, the researcher "generates or inductively develops a theory pattern of meaning"[2] from the participants.

The Rationale for Qualitative Research

I consider the qualitative research paradigm appropriate for this study because it will enable me to understand, describe, interpret, and examine the how and why of Igbo conversion to Islam. As Mugenda and Mugenda argued,

---

1. Creswell, *Research Design*, 9.
2. Creswell, 9.

qualitative research enables the researcher "to collect data and explain phenomenon more deeply and exhaustively."[3] The qualitative research paradigm helps to understand "the lived experiences of the people involved, or who were involved, with the issue that is being researched"[4] and it is suitable for investigating or studying "effective, emotional, and intense human experiences."[5] I consider it appropriate for this study because I am focusing on the lived experiences of Igbo converts to Islam. Since this study is not centered on hypotheses, variables, and measurement, the qualitative research design, which is personal in nature, is the most appropriate method to use. It should help me obtain an understanding of the phenomenon under study from the individual's perspective (individuals with the lived experience under investigation), to find out how people perceive their lives and the meaning they assign to their experience.

Qualitative research methods enable me to generate rich, detailed and valid (process) data that contributes to an in-depth understanding of the context. This kind of research design enables me to explain the behavior of the participants. It is advantageous in that it permits a researcher to go beyond the statistical results usually reported in quantitative research, helping to obtain an in-depth understanding of individual phenomena and the rich data from the experiences of the individuals. It can be disadvantageous because it does not produce generalizable data. However, since I am not concerned about testing hypotheses, generalizing the findings to a broader population, a quantitative method is not needed. "Instead the researcher's task is to present the experience of the people he or she interviews in compelling enough detail and in sufficient depth that those who read the study can connect to that experience, learn how it is constituted, and deepen their understanding of the issues it reflects."[6]

---

3. Mugenda and Mugenda, *Research Methods*, 197.
4. Green, "Lived World," 153.
5. Merriam, *Qualitative Research*, 26.
6. Seidman, *Interviewing as Qualitative Research*, 54.

Setting and Participants

Participants are the providers of information needed for the study, elicited orally or in writing. The participants for this study were thirty Igbo-born men and women who were Christians but have now converted to Islam. Their ages ranged from eighteen to sixty. These participants were contacted in five ways:

First, I went to the central mosques seeking help from the Chief Imams to provide names and contacts of converts. I introduced myself, my study, and the kind of assistance required from them. Some of these Chief Imams were also interviewed as they are converts to Islam. Some of those recommended by the Chief Imams were contacted through phone calls and personal visits.

Second, face-to-face recruitment in the mosques was adopted. I went to the mosques before and after prayer to personally recruit interviewees for the study. I approached them as they left the mosque or gathered outside the mosque.

Third, I used networks of women, local individuals, friends, and missionaries serving in the community. I received recommendations from these networks in contacting participants.

Fourth, converts already interviewed were asked to recommend other converts. I introduced myself to all participants with the help of the introductory letter obtained from Africa International University. I equally explained the content of the consent form to each participant and requested their consent by signing the form to participate in the study.

Fifth, two Igbo conversion narratives were obtained via the internet. These participants were interviewed by a newspaper house in Nigeria and their stories were published on the internet.

This study was carried out in a natural setting where the phenomenon was observed. The setting includes Enugu, Owerri, Enohia in Afikpo North, Nakanu in Afikpo and Afikpo town, all in Ebonyi State and Obollo Afor, Emilik Anu and Emiliki Ani, Ibagwa, Nsukka and Okija in Anambra. These sites were chosen in order to ascertain the reasons for conversion in the various areas of the Igbo region. Also, a majority of Igbo converts to Islam are located in some of these areas. At these sites I visited the Igbo Muslims in their mosques, shops, homes, and business centers to establish relationships and to interview them.

Sample Procedures

Sampling and selection are vitally important and strategic elements of qualitative research.[7] In qualitative research, Boyd feels a small sample size of between two and ten participants are sufficient while Creswell recommends "long interviews up to 10 people"[8] to ascertain in-depth understanding of the phenomenon. For this study, a sample of thirty participants was selected. The selection of the small sample size is purposive with criteria based on the phenomenon.

Purposeful sampling is widely used in qualitative research for the identification and selection of information-rich cases related to the phenomenon of interest. This means that the right kinds of people who have experienced the phenomenon are the best choices for the study. Since this study is concerned with the lived experience of a specific group of people, purposive sample is the most suitable. The thirty Igbo-born men and women who have converted from Christianity to Islam were purposively selected and the criteria for the selection were as follows:

1. The interviewee is ethnically Igbo and was a Christian living in Igboland, who has now converted to Islam.
2. The convert grew up as a Christian and then converted to Islam as an adult.
3. The convert is still a practicing Muslim.

Snowball sampling was also employed. This is asking a research participant to identify another potential participant that meets the research criteria. At the end of my interview with a participant, I ask him or her to identify or introduce me to another Igbo Muslim convert. Opportunistic sampling, which is using findings from one case in the selection of the next case, was also adopted.

I also used convenience sampling. While on a motorcycle riding to the bus station, I enquired of the motorcyclist if he knew of any Igbo who had converted from Christianity to Islam. He drove me to a market and pointed out to me a convert standing at a distance from us.

The reason for adopting these research sampling techniques was for easy accessibility of the right participants with the desired lived experience.

---

7. Mason, *Qualitative Researching*, 83.
8. Creswell, *Research Design*, 122.

Additionally, though the number of Igbo converting from Christianity to Islam is a growing phenomenon, the numbers are still relatively small among the Igbo general population. These sampling techniques were the best at identifying potential participants for the study.

Data Collection Procedures

Data collection for qualitative research often adopts in-depth face-to-face interviews with participants, a study of documents or documentaries about the people, and participant observation to observe the subjects in actual situations in which they engage in behaviors related to the phenomenon under investigation. For this study, the following data collection procedures were adopted.

Interview

An in-depth phenomenological face-to-face interview with Igbo converts to Islam was conducted. The interview was both semi-structured and unstructured. By semi-structured, I mean that I had limited questions in advance, but planned to ask follow-up questions based on answers to the prepared questions. The interview was also unstructured, as I proceeded according to Rubin and Ruben, where I had "a general topic in mind, but many of the specific questions will be formulated as the interview proceeds, in response to what the interviewee says."[9] General open-ended questions were asked, allowing participants to decide on how to respond and to share their experiences and their understanding assigned to those experiences in their own way with their own words.

Formal interviews were employed as well. This type of interview "usually occurs at an appointed time and results from a specific request to hold the interview."[10] With the permission of the interviewees, a time and venue convenient for the participant were used for the interview. The interviews lasted between forty-five minutes and two hours depending on the individual and the amount of information or experiences they had to share.

---

9. Rubin and Rubin, *Qualitative Interviewing*, 31.
10. Spradley, *Participant Observations*, 125.

The interview questions covered three important aspects of the life of the participant. The first aspect focused on their life history, second on the detailed experience relevant to the phenomenon under study, and finally the meaning the participant assigned to the experience. Though the primary source of data collection was interview, I also consulted available published records, including newspapers, magazines, and journals that may have contained helpful information. This was for the purpose of understanding previous works carried out on this issue; identifying any observed patterns and existing theories that could help in understanding the actions (changing process) of the participants. The interviews were conducted in the central mosques, homes, shops, and offices of the participants.

Observations

In addition to the interviews, observation was also employed in the collection of data. This is because "observations allow you as the researcher to immerse yourself into a social setting, enabling you to learn firsthand how the actions of participants are compatible with their words, the patterns of behaviors that exist, the expected and unexpected experiences that occur and how trust, relationships, and obligations with others are developed."[11] Observation enabled me to understand and interpret what conversion meant for each participant and search for patterns in their actions, feelings, and ideas that were reported. For example, some of the participants said one thing during their interview but did another in their real-life setting. Observation allowed me to compare what they said against what they did.

I used an observational form which was "a single page with a dividing line down the middle to distinguish descriptive notes from reflective notes which will include the researcher's personal thoughts, speculations, feelings, ideas, and prejudices during the research."[12] I made field notes of my observations of the attitudes of the participants that could not be captured in the interview recording, including their body gestures and my personal thoughts and understanding of such gestures. In my field notes, I endeavored to accurately document the date and time of the interview and the social environment,

---

11. Glesne, *Becoming Qualitative Researchers*, 10.
12. Creswell, *Research Design*, 198.

including the way in which participants interacted within their setting and their roles in that setting, as well as their behavior toward my questions.

Digital Recording

Before entering the field, qualitative researchers plan their approach to data recording. For me to work dependably and accurately with the words of the participants I converted them into a written text; the only reliable way for me to do that was to tape-record their original words. I tape-recorded every interview with the permission of each participant. At the end of the interview, I played the tape-recorded interview for some of them to hear our conversation. In one case, I sent a copy of the transcribed interview to the participant.

Data Analysis

According to Catherine Marshal and Gretchen B. Rossman typical analytic procedures fall into seven phases: organizing the data, immersion into the data, generating categories and themes, coding the data, offering interpretations through analytic memos, searching for alternative understandings, and writing the report or other format for presenting the study. I followed these seven steps in my analysis.[13]

Organizing the Data

I organized the data by transferring interviews collected onto my laptop and an external drive; the original copy was left on the digital recorder. I edited the field notes and logged them (including the interviews) according to a system by date, location, and participant. I read the interviews while still in the field to ensure that I could follow up on any omitted question. I noted if I missed a follow-up question while interviewing a participant, then I would visit them and get clarification.

I transcribed each recorded interview verbatim from the digital recording, including laughs, pauses, sighs, and interruptions as recorded. Transcribing the data myself enabled me to master the data, internalize it, and observe emerging themes. I created different folders to save the transcription according to location and date.

---

13. Marshall and Rossman, *Designing Qualitative Research*, 210–214.

Immersion in the Data

Intimate engagement with the data is essential; there is no substitute for this. I immersed myself with the data by reading, rereading and studying the data in order to observe emerging themes and patterns. Immersion in the data includes "moving deeper and deeper into understanding the data, representing the data, and making an interpretation of the larger meaning of the data."[14]

The data was reduced inductively, rather than deductively, by reading through the information to obtain a sense of the overall themes and patterns. In analyzing the data, I suspended and bracketed my judgment, presuppositions and views by not taking any position, either for or against the data collected, in order to understand the unique world and experience of the converts.

Coding the Data

Detailed analysis begins with a coding process, "the process of organizing the material into 'chunks' before bringing meaning to those 'chunks.'"[15] The data was coded by identifying certain patterns that answered the research questions and themes that emerged from the data. These patterns and themes were identified by closely reading the data, marking passages of interest, noting reoccurring ideas or language and labeling those passages through a word processing program. I created categories based on my research questions, then moved the codes into categories based on relatedness.

Interpreting the Findings

At this stage, I made meaning of the data collected from the participants based on what I had learned while conducting the interviews, studying the tran-scripts, and completing the literature review. I also discovered connective threads observed among the experiences of the participants that added support to my findings.

---

14. Creswell, *Qualitative, Quantitative and Mixed Methods*, 190.
15. Rossman and Rallis, *Learning in the Field*, 171.

Validating the Findings

This "means that the researcher determines the accuracy or credibility of the findings through strategies."[16] I adopted two strategies in determining the trustworthiness of this study. First is triangulation, which is substantiating a report by different individuals, sources or sites. I interviewed two brothers (older and younger) who are converts to Islam as well as many other individuals who have converted to Islam. The interview was conducted in various sites in Igboland like Ebonyi State, Enugu, Nsukka, Anambra, and Imo. Also I applied two data collection procedures (observation and in-depth interview) to ascertain accuracy in the data since the information was not to be drawn from a single participant, site and sources.

Second, I used an external auditor, my supervisor, to check the credibility of my study. He read, reviewed and commented on the strengths and weaknesses of the study, then suggested areas of improvement.

Reporting Findings

After coding, as well as identifying categories, themes and emerging patterns, I analyzed them for descriptions, I report the findings to my research questions. This was done by "constructing a narrative to explain what I have found and displaying findings in tables and figures."[17]

Site Entry

I entered into the settings through a pastor and missionaries serving at the various sites. These ministers connected me to the Chief Imams and individual Igbo Muslim converts, who then linked me to other converts. The Chief Imams were formal gatekeepers who gave me access to other converts, especially in the mosques, because that is where the Chief Imams and Muslim Converts were easily found.

Other informal gatekeepers were also contacted. In one community, a respected leader's participation in the study motivated others to participate when contacted. This particular leader was accessed through a Christian friend working in that community. I obtained a letter of introduction from

---

16. Creswell, *Educational Research*, 280.
17. Creswell, 274.

the Academic Dean of Africa International University, which introduced me and the purpose of the study. I gave the letter to every participant, along with a consent form to obtain their willingness to participate in the study.

Ethical Consideration

I sought the consent of the participants by obtaining informed consent for them to indicate their willingness to participant in the research. My consent form comprises the following: that they are participating in the research, the purpose of the research, the procedures of the research, the risk and benefits of the research, the voluntary nature of research participation, the participant's right to stop the research at any time, and the procedures used to protect confidentiality.

The purpose of the consent form was to provide transparency of the study to the participants in order to avoid suspicion and deception. For understanding and clarity, the consent form was explained to each participant at the beginning of the interview. All the participants consented, but were not interested in or willing to sign the form. In order to maintain privacy and anonymity of the interviewees none of their names are used in this work.

CHAPTER 4

Findings and Interpretation

Introduction

The purpose of this study was to identify the reasons Igbo Christians give for their conversion to Islam. So the fundamental question that influenced the collection of data and the subsequent analysis was, "what are the reasons Igbo Christian converts to Islam give for their conversion?" The data was collected through in-depth face-to-face interviews and observations.

The thirty Igbo Christian converts to Islam (twenty-three males and seven females) were interviewed in their mosques, homes, and shops. The presentation of findings is in accordance with the main research question and sub-research questions. The findings of the first two sub-research questions are presented first, followed by the main research question and third sub-research question being discussed together. This is because the answers to the third sub-research question were embedded in the answers generated from the main research question. The findings of the fourth sub-research question are presented last.

Findings

Sub-Research Question 1: What Are the Backgrounds (Social, Religious, and Familial) of the Converts?

Social background

The converts that participated in this study came from various regions in Igboland with various social backgrounds. For example, eleven converts were from Nsukka (Obolor Afor, Ibagwa, and Imilike included), eight converts from Owerri, seven from Afikpo, two from Enugu, one from Okija, and one from Asaba. This indicates that conversion to Islam is occurring in different parts of Igboland, not in just a few places. This finding seems to negate the popular assertion held by many Nigerians that conversion to Islam is only occurring in Afikpo and Nsukka. The Igbo in various Igboland areas are embracing Islam in their various localities.

The majority of participants were well educated while very few have little to no education. Their educational backgrounds included: one PhD holder, six graduate degree holders, fourteen senior secondary school certificate examination holders (SSCE), one junior secondary school holder (JSS3), two first school leaving certificate holders (FSLC), three with no educational qualifications, and three did not specify their educational qualifications. This indicates that conversion to Islam in Igboland cuts across educational backgrounds, from the most educated to the least educated.

Of the thirty converts interviewed, twenty-three were males and seven were females. The imbalance between the numbers of each gender is most likely a result of the method used in selecting participants. The interviews were conducted during Ramadan and in the mosques before and after prayers; fewer women than men joined in these activities. Again, those referred to me by the Chief Imams and a few other referrals were mostly men also. Furthermore, most female Muslims tend to be indigenous Igbo Muslims. The conversion phenomenon in Igboland seems to be occurring more among men than among women. Most importantly, all except one of the converted Igbo Christian women interviewed in this study converted to Islam as a requirement to marry their present husbands. This implies that these women may not have converted to Islam if not for marriage. Their conversion, therefore, was social pressure but existed and functioned as support. Of the research group, twenty-two converts were married, six unmarried, one engaged, and one did not specify his marital status.

Occupationally, the converts were gainfully employed by the government, self-employed in different businesses and trades, except two converts that were students and five retirees. They had a means of livelihood for themselves as well as their dependents. Their occupations ranged from business, tailoring, apprentice, Imams, students, civil servants, retirees, teachers, drivers, famers, medical doctor, P.R.O. Islamic community, and mechanic. The five retirees lived satisfactorily through farming, pension, and provision from their children. The apprentice was married, thus her husband catered for her. Though these converts may not be perceived as affluent, it does not suggest that they were desirous of material profit nor were they enjoying any special favors from Islam for converting. This finding indicates that their conversion to Islam was not likely influenced by a desire for material benefits or upward mobility, except in one incidence, since the majority already had jobs and families, and settled before their conversion to Islam. On the contrary, the benefits reported were peace of mind, contentment, fulfillment, and discovering the true worship of God. One convert claimed,

> Now I have peace of mind and satisfaction. If I don't have money now I'm not bothered; the little I have that can sustain me is enough for me. I cannot look for it by all means. So, the fulfillment I have in Islam is peace of mind and that *anya ukwu* (greediness) coveting to have what you don't have is no longer there.[18]

While another said,

> My condition did not change much but my own was to know the truth and what I was worshipping because then people were talking Jesus, Jesus, and Jesus; trinity, trinity, and trinity. I then understood that there is nothing like trinity. Nothing changed, in fact a lot of temptations started coming my way but since I found what I was looking for – the oneness of God. Some were saying there is God the son, God the father it made me decide that this [Islam] is the true way.[19]

Family background

All thirty converts interviewed came from families marked with tensions, problems and imbalance. For some, their fathers were absent in their lives, engaged in a promiscuous lifestyle, neglected them and were not religious. None of the converts had two committed Christian parents, so they were not fully socialized as children into Christianity. For example, three converts

---

18. Convert 7.
19. Convert 12.

came from animistic families where neither the true God nor church was emphasized. Two came from a family with dual religions – Christianity and African Traditional Religion. The father was the animist while the mother was a Christian; in such a situation the religion of the father would probably be followed. In such cases, the converts from these families were not properly and accurately socialized into Christianity. Two came from a family with dual denominations; Catholic and Christ Apostolic Church, and Anglican and Catholic Church. In both cases, the converts attended a denomination different from their parents' churches.

Those who had both parents practicing the same religion and attending the same denomination were twenty-three in number, but twenty-one of the families were not practicing their religion, and neither insisted that their children study the Bible nor attend church regularly. They were not rigid on inculcating Christian values into their children and did not take their religion seriously. Two of the converts came from a polygamous family, which was marked with tension, envy, unfair treatment, neglect, rivalry, and fighting for survival.

It is important to note that one of the two converts who reportedly came from a staunch Christian family, only converted to Islam with her husband after having lived together as Christians for a long while. One of these female converts married a Christian man and they lived as a Christian couple for several years until the husband was accused of embezzling church funds, which resulted in their defection to Islam. The second female convert from a staunch Christian family married a Muslim man and converted a few months after their marriage because she wanted religious homogeneity in her family. It is unclear why her staunch Christian family would agree to such a marriage. Perhaps, being fatherless, the mother may not have had strong resistance to this mixed marriage of a Muslim and a Christian. It is most likely appropriate to conclude that the majority of these converts are from families where the parents were not committed Christians, so they were not socialized as children into being Christians. However a good number of them became committed Christians despite their family religious backgrounds.

Religious background

The converts who participated in this study have varying backgrounds concerning their previous Christian religious beliefs and practices. Of the thirty converts, twenty-two stated that they were raised as Roman Catholics, four were Anglicans, one was from Assemblies, one from Redeemed Christian Church of God, one a Presbyterian, and one Pentecostal. This finding shows that most of the Christian converts to Islam are from the Roman Catholic Church. It suggests that there is more nominalism among the Catholics at present, having been one of the earliest denominations in Igboland.

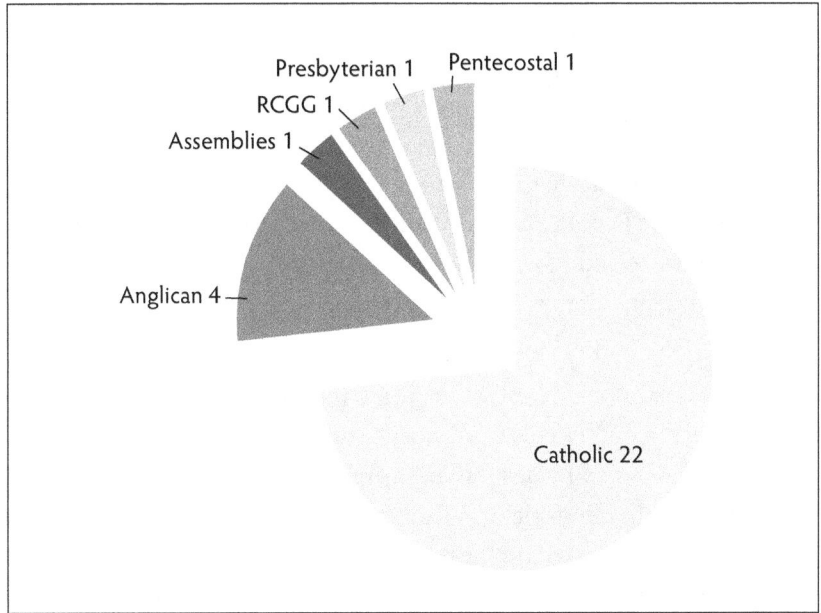

Figure 1. Church affiliation of participants

All thirty converts reported to have been Christians prior to conversion; twenty-eight of the thirty converts claimed to have been practicing Christians prior to conversion, while two reported that they were not practicing Christians prior to conversion. The converts are categorized into three categories: those who claimed to have been weak and nominal Christians, those who reported having been committed Christians prior to conversion, and those who stated they had been young prior to conversion, thus, knew little about Christianity.

The first category (fourteen converts) were those who considered themselves weak and nominal prior to conversion. These converts were nominal

Christians who attended church on Sundays only and were not seriously involved with other activities of the church. Religion for them was merely something called Christianity, Islam, or Hinduism, but they became transformed after their conversion to Islam. The following statements, from two of the converts, illustrate their nominalism:

> I was a member of the Anglican Church; that is where I was baptized. I was born and bred in that church as I found my parents, though they were not committed. They were not committed, but any time there was any festivity in the church, they would invite my father and he would go. But on Sundays, we did go there and worshipped.[20]

> I was a Christian but, as a Christian then, I could not understand it because I could not pray enough. Those I was walking with then, we would move from church to beer parlor. That time I drank a lot, I drank so much and womanized very well, I know how much I spent on drink and women then.[21]

For this first category, conversion means transformation, "taking of a new way of life in place of the old . . . a deliberate turning from indifference, a turning which implies a consciousness that a great change is involved, that the old was wrong and the new is right."[22] Transformation occurs in one of two ways; either turning to piety within the religion one adheres to, or exchanging the beliefs and practices of their religion for another. For these Igbo Christian converts, their transformation did not occur within Christianity but in a different religion – Islam. This seems to indicate that transformation can occur in any religion other than Christianity. Their transformation is evidenced by their changed lifestyles and commitment to God via praying five times a day, obeying the Qur'an, and participating in Ramadan; a change in their attitudes, habits and behavior. According to Kraft, transformation ought to result in a change in allegiance (faith commitment to God) which leads to a change in worldview, and in turn leads to a change in attitude, habits, and behavior.[23]

---

20. Convert 25.
21. Convert 10.
22. Nock, *Conversion*, 7.
23. Gilliland and Kraft, *Appropriate Christianity*, 348–349.

This type of change was evidenced in the converts' lives. Their change aligns with Baer's definition of conversion as well,

> conversion is a decision or experience followed by a gradually unfolding, dynamic process through which an individual embarks on religious transformation. This can entail intensification on belief and practice of one's own religion moving from one level of observation to another, or exchanging the beliefs and practices in which one was raised for those of another religious tradition. In both cases, a person becomes someone else because his or her internal mind-set and/or external actions are transformed.[24]

It appears evident that these Igbo Christian converts became transformed after conversion to Islam.

The second category (thirteen converts) includes those that considered themselves committed Christians while in Christianity. They had a clear understanding of the evangelistic perception of what it is to be a Christian, some had even accepted Jesus Christ as their Lord and Savior, attended church regularly, including weekly services, were baptized (infant baptism), received the Eucharist, participated in the activities of the church, contributed toward the projects of the church, belonged to one or two groups in the church, taught catechism, or were being trained to become a Reverend Father. These converts (except two males) became disenchanted or disillusioned and changed to Islam. Their disillusionment was not with the theological beliefs or practices of Christianity, but with the attitude and behavior of some Christians and pastors. A convert stated his disenchantment with the church thus:

> Then they [Christians] believe that Jesus is their Lord and personal Savior and that He is the Son of God. So that as a Christian you need to believe in Jesus and as well be born again. Yeah, I believed in that and I was in the intercessory arm of the church.[25]

---

24. Baer, *Honored by the Glory of Islam*, 13.
25. Convert 22.

Another said,

> I was baptized, confirmed, and received Eucharist in the Catholic Church. I was one of those who instituted carols during Christmas in my village Umuomi Uzoagba. My life has been pure in Christianity, I was a man servant, and my Reverend father used to call me, "Anthony, talk to them" [i.e.] the men servants who were behaving . . . their behavior was rubbish. Reverend father would call me to talk to them because of my character and my quality.[26]

For these Igbo converts conversion meant and means transformation; exchanging their Christian beliefs and practices for another religion. They observe and obey the Qur'an teachings, observe Ramadan, engage in *da'wah*, serve as Chief Imams, pray regularly, and so on. Thus, their conversion seems to be a carry-over of their religious commitment from Christianity to Islam; no new transformation occurred. The only change is just the exchange of beliefs and practice to a different religion. The converts' rejection of their parents' religion did not imply rejection of their belief in God because they converted to another religious alternative that still believes in God.

The third category covers those three converts that considered themselves young when they were Christians, and therefore knew little or nothing about Christianity. A convert reported that "when I was a Christian I would say it was during my childhood though I was not a stubborn or rebellious person right from that time."[27] Another stated,

> When my parents were Christians (they still are) at that time I did not know much, I was still a young, growing boy. So, I will not talk much concerning Christians. [At] that time, I was about fourteen years. At least a child of about fourteen years [at] that time knows nothing. Not that he knows nothing, but he knows nothing concerning religion.[28]

---

26. Convert 16.
27. Convert 12.
28. Convert 4.

In this category, conversion means the same thing as the first category above, transformation. They are now changed and transformed people, just like their counterparts in category one.

The narrative across all three categories of converts appears to insinuate that the effect of Christianity in Igbo society is reducing. Furthermore, the church seems to be losing members, not to a different denomination, but to a different religion without being aware of it. Also, this narrative suggests that the church is losing its influence over their people.

In concluding the background analysis of all the converts, there is no concrete or conclusive demographic pattern to describe them. They came from different Christian affiliations, different parts of Igboland, different educational backgrounds, and different professions, as well as being of a different gender. This finding reveals that conversion from Christianity to Islam occurs across age, profession, gender, education, and denominations. The table below summarizes the descriptive elements of all the converts.

Table 2. Summary of the descriptive elements of the converts

Partici-pants	Educational qualification	Occupation	Marital status	Religious Background of family	Church affiliation prior Conversion	Gender
1	None	Business	Married	Dual (Christian & ATR)	Catholic	F
2	SSCE	Retiree	Unspecified	Christian	Catholic	M
3	SSCE	Staff	Unmarried	Christian	Catholic	M
4	FSLC	Tailor	Married	Christian	Catholic	M
5	SSCE	Business	Married	Christian	Catholic	F
6	Graduate	Business	Married	Christian	Catholic	M
7	SSCE	Retiree	Married	Christian	Anglican	M
8	Unspecified	Preacher/farmer	Married	Christian	Catholic	M
9	SSCE	Trader	Engaged	ATR	Assemblies	F
10	None	Mechanic	Married	Dual (Christian & ATR)	Catholic	M
11	FSLC	Driver	Married	Christian	Catholic	M
12	SSCE	Business	Married	Christian	Catholic	M
13	Graduate	Business	Married	Dual (Catholic & CAC)	Catholic	F
14	SSCE	Retiree	Married	Christian	Presbyterian	M
15	SSCE	Retiree	Married	Christian	Anglican	M
16	Graduate	Business	Single	Christian	Catholic	M
17	Graduate	Teacher	Single	Christian	Catholic	M
18	Unspecified	Farmer	Married	Christian	Catholic	M
19	JSS3	Apprentice	Married	Christian	Catholic	F
20	SSCE	Unspecified	Single	Christian	Pentecostal	M
21	SSCE	PRO	Married	Christian	Catholic	M

Partici-pants	Educa-tional qualifica-tion	Occupation	Marital status	Religious Background of family	Church affiliation prior Conversion	Gen-der
22	SSCE	Imam/farmer	Married	ATR	Catholic	M
23	SSCE	Student	Single	Christian	RCCG	F
24	SSCE	Civil servant	Married	Dual (Ang. & Catholic)	Anglican	F
25	Graduate	Accountant	Married	Christian	Anglican	M
26	SSCE	Business	Married	ATR	Catholic	M
27	None	business	Married	Christian	Catholic	M
28	PhD	Scientist/Da'wee	Married	Christian	Catholic	M
29	Unspec-ified	Retiree	Married	Christian	Catholic	M
30	Graduate	Student	Single	Christian	Catholic	M

Sub-Research Question 2: What Are the Stages of Their Conversion?

Gerlach and Hine expounded upon a profound conversion model based on their survey of Pentecostalism in the United States.[29] They observed seven identifiable steps in the commitment process that a potential convert undergoes before embracing a new religion. According to them, a person must have (1) initial contact with a participant, (2) a focus of needs through demonstration, (3) re-education through group interaction, (4) decision and surrender, (5) a commitment event, (6) testimony to the experience, and (7) group support for changed cognitive and behavioral patterns. Lewis Rambo, an influential writer on religious conversion, also developed a popular seven step conversion model based on his research: (1) context, (2) crisis, (3) quest, (4) encounter, (5) interaction, (6) commitment, and (7) consequences.[30] These

---

29. Gerlach and Hine, *People, Power, Change*.
30. Rambo, "Psychology of Conversion."

models were presented in detail in chapter 2, now their applicability to the conversion process of the Igbo Christian converts is discussed here.

The first process, initial contact with a participant, was reported by twenty-three converts. All twenty-three of the converts reported that their initial contact with Islam was through a Muslim. These initial contacts with Muslims by participants I have classified into five categories. First are those who came into contact with Islam through their spouses (five females). Second are those who came into contact with Islam through family members or relatives, this includes brothers, brother-in-laws, kinsmen, and a maternal uncle. The third group came into contact with Islam through friends, colleagues, or neighbors. The fourth came into contact with Islam through a boss. Finally, the fifth group includes those who came into contact with Islam through unique processes, including direction from God via dreams; one convert reported this process. According to him, "No Muslim knew me before I entered Islam; any Muslim that knows me knew me when I entered Islam. It is God that brought me into Islam." Through a stranger, one convert reported that he and his brother were accused of killing their parents through witchcraft when they were children. Due to this, they were maltreated, so they left home not knowing where they were going. A couple met them in another town crying and carried them to the government. After nine months under the government's custody, with no one reporting them missing or claiming them, they were given to the couple that found them. This couple became their foster parents and introduced them to Islam. Through Mankaranta (qur'anic evening school), one convert explained that when he was growing up, he would see children in the evening learning the Qur'an. He joined them, and over time embraced Islam. Therefore, Gerlach and Hine's first stage of contact with a Muslim participant is highly evident in the Igbo Christian conversion process to Islam.

However, seven (six males and one female) interviewees' conversion stage began with context, which implies that they were disenchanted with their context, religion, culture, society or personal environment. They had crises such as frustration for lack of employment, maltreatment of Christians, or sickness. Of these, two expressed having had a quest for meaning and purpose in life. Looking at Gerlach and Hine, as well as Rambo's models at this stage contact, the first stage of Gerlach and Hine model was reported by twenty-three converts while Rambo's model was reported by seven converts.

The second process, focus of needs through demonstration, was reported by four converts (three males and one female). They reported to have observed positive change, fulfillment, and seriousness with the things of God in the life of their Muslim friends, relatives, colleagues, or neighbors. For example, one convert stated, "I started observing some characteristics in their [Muslims friends] lives which are quite different from mine: they were not living as sinful as I was. After a while, I started liking Muslims, and no one preached to me. It was just their character that influenced me to join Islam."[31] This shows that Islam possesses power to change a life; Muslims are engaging in *da'wah* through their lifestyle; Christians observe how Muslims live their lives; and Igbo Christians have relationships with Igbo Muslims.

In the third stage, re-education through group interaction, seventeen converts stated that they were taught Islamic values, ideology, beliefs, and practices. They began practicing Islamic teachings, like praying five times daily, and observing Islamic laws, such as abstinence from drinking alcohol, smoking, and eating pork. They also accepted Islamic ideology on the monotheistic nature of Allah. A convert stated that "they [Muslims] began explaining some certain things [about Islam] to me, so one day I just decided to embrace Islam."[32] Another convert reported that his brother in-law, whom he was living with, taught him the history of Islam. At this stage, Gerlach and Hine postulated that if external relationships are neutral or weak, the potential convert will quickly bond with the new religion. This appears to be applicable in this study as some converts reported that they had stopped attending church for about a year and others stated they had no strong ties with Christians, except their childhood friends. This neutral state, or weak bonds with Christians or the church, resulted in easy abdication to Islam. One convert narrated his experience as follows:

> During that period. I was not even going to any church. In short, since I went to Lagos, I never attended church because my church was not around. When he [a Muslim friend] was close to me, he was telling me about Islam, teaching me how

---

31. Convert 13.
32. Convert 13.

> to read Qur'an in Arabic, and telling me that Islam is the right road to worship God. During that time he had pulled me down.[33]

The converts were re-educated through preaching, teaching, explanations, and being given materials to read about Islam. The outcome of their re-education was decision and surrender to Islam. This stage parallels Rambo's interaction stage.

The fourth stage, decision and surrender, was present in the narrative of all the thirty converts (twenty-three males and seven females). At the end of the converts' study and learning about Islam, observation of the Muslim lifestyle, and on occasion even coercion, they surrendered their old identity and embraced Islam. The following narratives support this point:

> He [a Muslim] supplied me with textbooks and after reading the textbooks, because I had my belief then as a Christian, I have my own belief. So after reading the textbooks and those things in the textbooks that aligned with my own belief, I said, "Okay, this particular religion I will give it a try let me see if it's actually the religion of God."[34]

> Then I came back here [to the mosque]; I was with him [a friend]. So many of his Muslim brothers were forcing me to convert to Islam. I said, "no." So they were like trying to push me for roughly a month, and then one day I just decided to make up my mind and embrace the religion.[35]

These reports show that converts reach a point where they surrender their old identity in their conversion journey. This stage parallels Rambo's commitment stage.

The fifth process, the commitment event, all thirty converts performed some rituals to symbolize their turning away with finality from things and people associated with their former roles and associations as Christians. This event included taking of *Shahada* (public declaration of their acceptance of Islam), change of name, and induction through taking a bath (the Igbo converts call this bath baptism). This parallels Rambo's commitment stage.

---

33. Convert 9.
34. Convert 11.
35. Convert 3.

The sixth stage, testifying of the experience, was absent in the converts' conversion process narratives. Although this stage appears absent in the data, since I did not ask any question specifically on this topic, it could still be present, but has gone unreported.

The seventh stage, group support for changed cognitive and behavioral patterns, appears to be present in the experience of all the converts. Rambo termed this stage "consequence." The converts reported that their conversion resulted in negative consequences from family members and their society which included: ridiculing, threats, insults via name calling like *onye Hausa* ("Hausa person"), *ndi allakuba* ("those who heat heads on the ground"); rejection, quarrels, hatred, estrangement, deprivation, isolation, keeping malice, attempted murder, abandonment, dissolution of marriage, fighting, enmity, perceived as an enemy, anger, and others. Sebastian and Parameswara's typologies of interaction were adopted to illustrate the consequences of the converts' conversion to Islam.

Sebastian and Parameswaran discovered four typologies of interaction that exist between ethnic Chinese who adopted an alien faith, Hare Krishna, and their family members. These are classified as contentious, neutral, accommodative, and supportive. The interaction between the converts in this study and their families, as well as society, was described according to these typologies.

Contentious interaction

Of the thirty converts in this study, twenty (nineteen males and one female) reported to have had contentious interaction (characterized by a pervading sense of anger and bitterness maintained over long periods of time) with family members after conversion. Below are few examples.

> Even my own family hates me because I embraced Islam, because they followed me and joined CMS. They said that I am *onye Hausa* ("Hausa person"), they called me Hausa that I am *onye Hausa* that we are not related, because of what? Because I embraced Islam! When there is a function in our family, they don't inform me. I just refrain from seeing them.[36]

---

36. Convert 14.

They [his parents] weren't happy at the first stage. They poured chemicals into my bathing water, unknown to me, and after bathing, my body was no longer the same. Even presently, you can see some [showing me his burnt skin from the acidic water] you can see my skin, this is what I went through. I was hospitalized for a good year. If you look at my neck [showing me and I saw it for myself], I could not see nor talk. Even my hair, do you know blue band butter? My head was just like that. There was no single hair then on my head, it was bald. I cannot easily turn my head until now due to the damage of the acid. So, I went through a lot. Look at my finger nails [showing me] everything got peeled off. So many things; I know what I passed through.[37]

My wife abandoned me and the children, and ran away because of my conversion. It was not easy: the club we used to attend, the social life we lived, the drinks we drank and the rest of the things are forbidden by Islam. I may not say that why my wife left me is because of Islam, but it's partly because of Islam, because the money was no longer coming in as before because in Islam we don't take any money anyhow. No haram money, the money you worked for, all the beer parlors we had, I closed them down, so she could not stay without money. Her name is *ogbenyeanu* [a woman a poor man can't marry]. So she had to opt out and married another Christian. It got even worse when, as a machine journalist, I started preaching on television and radio, trying to present what Islam is all about. In fact, everybody hated me, not only my people, but everybody who knew me up till when I packed in here. So the situation wasn't easy.[38]

They [the parents] didn't welcome it; they said that I have abandoned their own religion, that it is a mistake on my own side. But I tried to convince them that Allah has granted me the knowledge which has not reached them, and that I have read and heard what they have not heard or read before. So that is

---

37. Convert 20.
38. Convert 24.

how, in fact, it brought a slight enmity between us until death. Until they died they were still bearing grudges against me for abandoning the religion they chose for me.[39]

Neutral interaction

Of the converts four (three males and one female) reported that their family members' interaction with them was neutral. They just ignored them and allowed them to practice their newfound religion. One convert stated that, "they [the family members] did nothing; they have no option, and they can't dictate to me, as I am a matured man. They cannot dictate to me, there is a stage you yourself will reach you cannot be dictated to."[40] The female in this category stated, "my family was just saying that they don't like my conversion."[41] The family members in this category were neutral because the converts were of age to decide, though they frowned upon it.

Accommodative interaction

Similar to above, four converts (three males and one female) reported that their families are comfortable with their new religion, provided it does not create a rift between these women and their husbands or family members. For example, one convert stated that her family admonished her to do whatever she needs to do to avoid having problems with her husband. Another stated, "Thank God our people here know more about Islam than Catholicism. They believe that Islam is a religion, but some people believe that Islam is a tribe, so when they see a Muslim they call the person *onye Hausa*. We don't believe in that."[42]

Supportive interaction

This reflects the interaction between two converts and their families. One convert reported that his mother was supportive of his conversion and she eventually converted to Islam before her death. "My mother supported me. I went home and told my mother to do *kalimashal* [confession of Islamic faith]

---

39. Convert 25.
40. Convert 13.
41. Convert 8.
42. Convert 10.

and she did. My mother loved me [smiling] but eventually she died."[43] The other stated that "My mom was an animist but she later embraced Islam. She was a Muslim."[44]

In some cases, converts keep their conversion secret. One convert withheld the news of his conversion from his parents, but disclosed it to his senior brother. "My family, anyway my dad, is not aware because some people told me that I should not relate it to him, so that I will not start having some indifference with them. It is only my senior brother that is aware, and his reactions are not too bad."[45]

The kind of interaction that exists between converts and family depends on the causal condition: family-convert relationship, religious identity of family members, convert's habitation, and family members' perceptions of the convert's religion.[46] The following figure summarizes these relationship typologies between converts and their families.

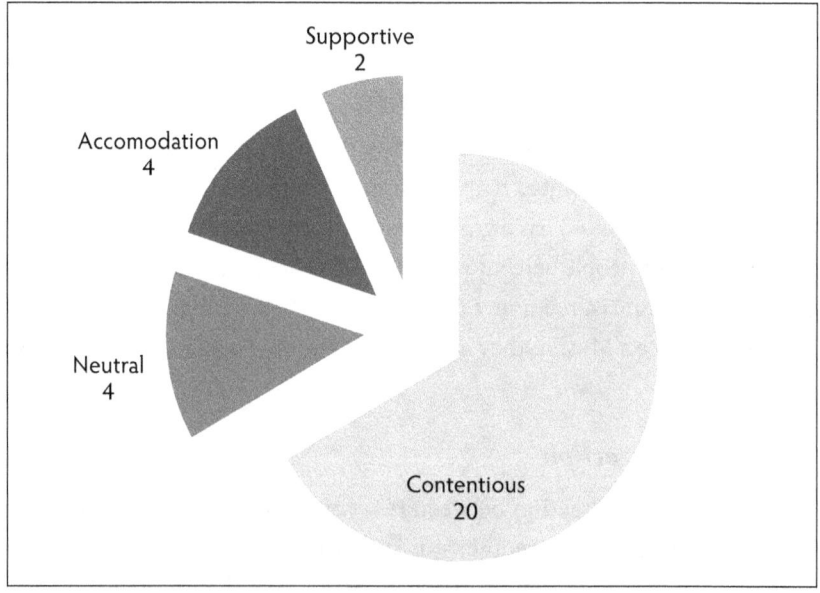

Figure 2. Interaction typology between converts and families

---

43. Convert 16.
44. Convert 22.
45. Convert 30.
46. Parameswaran and Sebastian, "Conversion and the Family," 350.

Out of Gerlach and Hine's seven steps stage model of conversion process, six were applicable to this study and all of Rambo's seven stages of process were present in this study, but in fewer cases. From Rambo's stages model, that was applied to this study, five out of seven paralleled Gerlach and Hine's five of the seven conversion processes reported in this study. So, when these paralleled stages from both scholars are considered, it indicates that only five of their conversion processes are significant and applicable to this study. However, Gerlach and Hine's were reported, or experienced, by more converts as tables 3 and 4 below illustrate.

So the difference between these scholars' models is that Rambo's stages one and two were absent in Gerlach and Hine's. Gerlach and Hine's stage four and six were also absent in Rambo's stage model. In conclusion, I found most of these scholars' models applicable in the Igbo conversion process to Islam.

Table 3. Stages of the converts' conversion process

Stages	Gerlach and Hine	No of converts	Rambo	No of converts
1	Initial contact with a person	23	Context	7
2	Focus of need through demonstration	4	Crisis	6
3	Re-education through group interaction	17	Quest	2
4	Decision and surrender	30	Encounter	7
5	Commitment event	30	Interaction	3
6	Testifying of the experience	0	Commitment	7
7	Group support for changed cognitive and behavioral patterns	30	Consequences	30

Table 4. Parallel conversion process of Gerlach and Hine and Rambo

Stages	Gerlach and Hine	Rambo
1 = Rambo	Nil	Context
2 = Rambo	Nil	Quest
1 = Gerlach Hine & Rambo	Initial contact with a person	Encounter
2 = Gerlach Hine & Rambo	Focus of need through demonstration	Crisis
3 = Gerlach/Hine & Rambo	Re-education through group interaction	Interaction
4 = Gerlach/Hine & Rambo	Decision and surrender	Nil
5 = Gerlach/Hine	Commitment event	Commitment
6 = Gerlach/Hine	Testifying of the experience	Nil
7 = Gerlach/Hine & Rambo	Group support for changed cognitive and behavioral patterns	Consequences

Main Research Question: What Are the Igbo Converts' Reasons for Their Conversion to Islam?

In this section, both sub-research question three (Which conversion motifs are involved in their conversion to Islam?) and the main research question are answered because the answers to sub-research question three were embedded in the findings of the main research question.

Lofland and Skonovd developed six conversion motifs that lead to conversion, through their research experience with students of new religious movements. These motifs include intellectual, mystical, experimental, affectional, revival and coercive. Each of these motifs is characterized by five independent elements: (1) degree of social pressure (2) temporal duration (3) level of affective arousal (4) affective content and (5) belief-participation sequence.

These conversion motifs were appraised in this study and their applicability examined. Applying these conversion motifs to this study, the Igbo Christian converts to Islam experienced all the elements except revivalist.

Intellectual and affectional were dominant while mystical, experimental and coercive were extremely uncommon. Two other reasons emerged that were not covered by Lofland and Skonovd's theory: upward mobility and a place to serve as minister and still get married. Figure 3 demonstrates this:

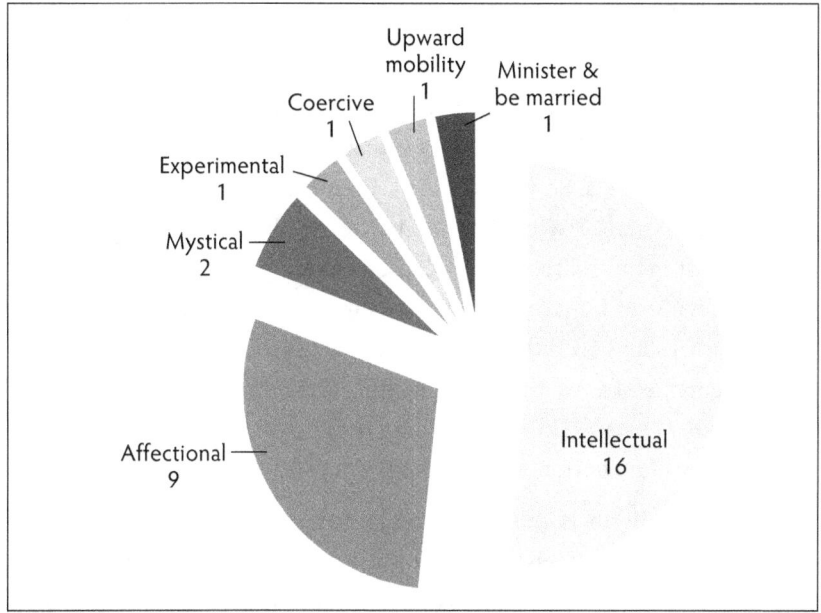

Figure 3. Conversion motifs of the converts

The intellectual motif was claimed in sixteen cases. Of the interviewees seven (six males and one female) reported to have read Islamic books, materials, or Qur'an and listened to preaching and discovered that Islam is reasonable, rational, and logical to them. They perceived many doctrinal issues to be irrational, unreasonable and illogical, such as: the Sonship of Jesus (Jesus being the Son of God); the Trinity; original sin; mediatory role of Jesus; Bible being changed over time; contradictions in biblical accounts (especially in the Gospels); division of the Bible into Old and New Testaments; Jesus being God; God speaks to people in the Bible indirectly through authors (e.g. letter to the Philippians, Romans); and denominationalism in Christianity (they reported that in Islam you just have Muslims, there is nothing like Anglican, Roman Catholic, Jehovah Witnesses). "When you report to be a Christian then you are asked, 'Which church? Is the church divided?,' they would ask."[47] Islam, on the other hand, they explained as reasonable, rational, and logical because it enables you understand that God is one not two, the Qur'an is incorruptible, God speaks directly to you in the Qur'an, you worship God directly, not through anybody, it explains how God cannot have a son, the oneness of Allah, and the teachings of Islam as simple and reasonable.

> You know, the New Testament does not teach completely how Christ came to that divinity state, but the Qur'an helped us understand that Christ's divinity is just like a messenger, like all other prophets. So when I saw it, I realized that there is a difference there. We in Christianity, we are almost worshipping Christ in an indirect way because in every prayer, we say, "In the name of Jesus," which in the Qur'an it is not like that. The Qur'an starts everything with the name of God, *bisimillahi*, "In the name of God, the most gracious, the most merciful," that is how we start. This thing touched me very well, and I said [to myself] I better follow that way.[48]

The second item is the irrational and the hypocritical life of some Christians and pastors. Five converts (four males and one female) asserted that their conversion to Islam was due to the attitude of Christians, such as: false accusations of embezzling church funds, hypocrisy, refusal to assist the needy, lies, maltreatment, greed, poisoning, flamboyant burial rites, refusal to bury the deceased who were not up to date on their dues, excessive demand of money by the church, flamboyant lifestyles of pastors, usurping of church members, and the prosperity gospel in the church. One convert reported that she abdicated from Christianity "because of the way the Christians treated my husband, because of the Christians' attitude towards my husband."[49] Others asserted that,

> I observed different characteristics and attitudes among our people; there is no truth in them. In the kindred meeting, we agreed that this is how this thing will be handled 1, 2, 3, [and]

---

47. Convert 16.
48. Convert 7.
49. Convert 5.

the decision is changed. When we now reconvene to execute the decision, people will divide and disagree. Is this what is written in the Bible? Back then, I was not a Muslim and did not read the Qur'an. Their attitude is not biblical; it is not in the Holy Book [the Bible]. There is no truth in you people. These attitudes of my people overwhelmed me, so I went to Okoro telling him that I want to become a Muslim.[50]

If you attend church one-hundred times per day but fail to pay your dues, when you are in need, they will forget you. If you participate in the building of the church and other activities, but you fail to pay your dues, they will forget other good things you have done in the church. They are demanding dues even if it is N200.00 that is contributed, its mandatory that you pay yours; they don't care whether you have it or not. What a rich man pays is what a poor person will pay. When a Christian dies, the record book will be brought to find out if the deceased was up-to-date in his payment of dues and they know the deceased was a poor person. This deceased person was committed in the church and participated in all the activities of the church, but if this deceased person has unpaid debt, the church will refuse to bury the remains. It is now the animists/traditional people who will come to bury the person. Is this good? The traditional people will say, we can't leave the corpse since the church won't bury it because he was not paying his dues, let us bury him.[51]

They stated that the Christians do not live out what they preach but Muslims, on the contrary, live out what they preach.

The third issue the converts mentioned was the greater ethical, moral, and consistent lifestyle of Muslims, as stipulated in the Qur'an. Four converts reported that they were convinced to embrace Islam because of the lifestyle Muslims demonstrated in their, seriousness to follow the things of God (praying five times daily), their neatness and purity,[52] their fear of God,

---

50. Convert 18.

51. Convert 15.

52. This purity is outward cleanness like washing oneself before and after sexual intercourse, abstinence from drinking alcoholic beverages and eating of pork, touching the

their love for one another, truthfulness, and good character. One convert stated, "I started observing some characteristics in their lives which were quite different from mine; they were not living as sinful as I was. After a while, I started liking Muslims. No one preached to me; it was just their characters that influenced me to join Islam."[53] Another convert posited,

> It's just that I saw the seriousness when it comes to the things of God compared to we Christians' seriousness to the things of God. Because in Islam what I observed is this: Someone will leave whatsoever thing he is doing – your business, your job, whatsoever thing you are doing at that point in time whenever you hear the call for prayer. You will rush down to the mosque to make sure that you give what belongs to God at that point in time. But in Christendom, there are people that know they are to go to church around seven o'clock in the morning, and maybe close by twelve noon you see some people coming, by 11:50 a.m.[54]

As noted in these reports, the converts in this category did not experience any predisposing tension, crisis, trauma, spiritual condition to know God better, social pressure, emotional feeling of hopelessness, nor negative economic situation to drive them to conversion to Islam. Rather, it was a conscious and intentional decision after a long period of study of Islamic materials, and careful observation of the character of Muslims as compared to Christians and the church, that they came to their conclusions. There was no external force, enticement or inducement involved in their decision for Islam. This finding seems to negate the popular assertion that the Igbo are converting to Islam due to economic benefits or material enticements. The majority of the converts were established in their professions and businesses prior to their conversion to Islam, thus, they had no need for monetary or economic improvements in their situations motivating their conversions. This finding also indicates that the Igbo are delving into religions other than Christianity. Furthermore, this finding appears to negate Okorocha's assertion that the Igbo embrace religion that will usher them into a viable life (increase

---

Qur'an and entering the mosque during menstruation, washing oneself after defecation, ablution before prayers.

53. Convert 10.
54. Convert 20.

in social status and better economic situation in life) because these converts to Islam were already professionals in their occupations, established, and married with children prior to conversion. It is true that this motive was present in the Igbo conversion to Christianity, but it appears absent in these converts explanations of why they converted.

The converts' reports also appear to lend credence to Lofland-Skonovd's theory that there is "little or no external pressure involved, the event occurs over a number of weeks or months – a period characterized as 'medium' in length. The convert-in-process is affectively aroused, but the emotional level is far from ecstatic. The emotional tone of the experience seems best characterized as one of 'illumination.'"[55] This finding corresponds with Mehmedoglu and Kim's study of twenty-seven Korean converts to Islam. They observed that "their conversions were the result of fully conscious choices made after careful examination and consideration of the alternatives."[56] The present findings of this study also parallel the research findings of Dikki on eleven Kenyan Christian converts to Islam. He discovered that their conversion was purely intellectual with no material enticement involved.[57] Furthermore, these findings demonstrate that the conversion process is gradual as the majority of the converts spent a considerable amount of time in reading, observing and comparing the two religions before making their decisions to convert.

It is also important to note that Islam is a religion of works and observation of rules, unlike Christianity where work is blended with grace. Some studies of conversions to Christianity reveal that Muslims are equally converting to Christianity for intellectual reasons. In such studies, intellectual, affectional and revivalist motifs are found to play a significant role. The majority of converts in this study report focusing on the observation of Islamic rules, the do's and dont's, and this is what they present to other Igbo who show interest in Islam. For example, one convert reported,

> They were more than twenty that came to my house indicating interest to embrace Islam, and I told them that there is nothing they will ask you to bring. What will debar you is not keeping the law; Muslims pray five times daily, which is the law God

---

55. Lofland and Skonovd, "Conversion Motifs," 376.
56. Kim and Mehmedoglu, "Conversion Motifs," 132.
57. Dikki, "Missiological Study of Islamic Strategies," iv.

gave, and you will be asked about it when you die. Muslims do not drink, Muslims pray five times daily, Muslims do not belong to age groups. This is what is enticing them away from their religion.[58]

The second reason for the Igbo conversion to Islam is the affectional motif. Nine converts (four males and five females) reported that their reason for conversion was affectional. Their decision to convert was influenced by opinions and demand of friends and neighbors, who were already practicing Muslims. For the four males, the kindness, love, and care from Muslims, as well as healing received from a Muslim, endeared them to Islam. For instance, One convert returned with his wife to his home town after the demise of his father to assume the inheritance of his late father. Being the only son left with much land and property, he was poisoned. According to him, he vomited blood frequently, which incapacitated him for four years. He tried both Western and traditional medicines to no avail; he resigned himself to the fate of waiting for death. A friend of his introduced him to a Muslim, who is Alhaji from a southern part of Nigeria, residing in Igboland. This Alhaji assured the convert that he could cure him through pray and a day was fixed for the prayer. While in the house of the Alhaji, about 12:00 a.m., the Alhaji woke him up and they began praying. In response to this he said, "I never knew how Muslims prayed. He was hitting his head on the floor, kneeling down, standing up and I was just imitating whatever he did."[59] At 3:00 a.m. sharp, the Alhaji wrote something on the black board from the Qur'an which he washed off with water. This water was then poured into a star beer bottle, reaching only half full in the bottle, and the convert was asked to drink it for forty days:

> He told me that I should drink one glass cup every morning for forty days starting the next day. (The size of the glass cup was half the usual glass cup.) So I asked him, "oga, how can I drink this thing for 40 days? It will finish. Let me take a smaller quantity so that it can serve for forty days." He said, "no," that I must fill it. So I went home. Every day I took one short [glass]

---

58. Convert 18.
59. Convert 29.

> and drank and the quantity was still at the same level as of the day it was given to me until the thirtieth day, it began reducing, reducing and reducing until that fortieth day it finished. Do you understand? It [the bleeding] went final [ended], I did not feel anything again. I was cured finally and completely. That is how [and why] I embraced Islam.[60]

This convert has remained a committed and dedicated practicing Muslim to this day. He vows to die a Muslim. "I will not leave Islam; I will practice Islam until my death."[61]

Another convert reported that Muslims are upright, and award scholarship to study in Saudi Arabia, which was what influenced his decision to convert.

> I had to break from them [the church] and join the Islamic religion because they do physically things, they do what I like, they are upright, they hardly commit offence. They treated me warmly, my children are members too and everything is free, education free, everything is free. They don't pay school fees; they educate you up to Mecca level, medina. Some of our children, many of them are there in Mecca medina University.[62]

The four converts in this category were impressed by the kindness of Muslims and the gift of healing received from a Muslim as well. This finding indicates that the Islamic strategy of love, kindness, and care are effective. It also shows that the method of healing adopted in Islam, like in the above case, is effective.

The five female converts in this category converted before marriage in order to marry their spouses. One convert was engaged to marry a Muslim man and her engagement occurred after her conversion. This is in accordance with the Qur'an's teaching that Muslims do not engage in marital relationships with a non-believer unless the potential spouse becomes a Muslim. "Do not marry Unbelieving women (idolaters), until they believe: A slave woman who believes is better than an unbelieving woman, even though she allures you. Nor marry (your girls) to unbelievers until they believe: A man slave who believes is better than an unbeliever even though he allure(s) you."(Q. 2:

---

60. Convert 29.
61. Convert 29.
62. Convert 14.

221). Islam is very strict, tight, and uncompromising on mixed marriage. This strictness is strong for the non-Muslim man who must convert in order to marry a Muslim woman. This challenges the popular tradition that a woman leaves her religion to adopt that of her husband. In Islam, the reverse is the case, the non-Muslim man must renounce his original religion and accept Islam before he can marry a Muslim woman. This is due to Islam's strong emphasis on the headship of the man.

As the head of the family, the man determines the direction of the home. So, allowing his daughters to marry a non-Muslim man means the girl will reject her faith and embrace that of the husband's, which Islam does not tolerate. However, in this study, those in this category were women and their conversion was therefore associated with marrying a Muslim partner. This may also have been possible because of the traditional subordinate role of women and the Igbo custom that a woman has no religion until she is married. I observed this customary belief in some converts' narrative. For example, one convert said, "I got married and joined my husband in Islam. When you are married, you follow your husband to his church you don't join another church. So, I joined him in his religion."[63] Another said, "He is the one I joined to embrace Islam. You know that women don't have a choice, it is your husband that you will follow."[64]

This finding is similar to the findings of Kadijah Mohd Khambali,[65] who worked among the Sabah people of Malaysia. She discovered that interfaith marriage and conversion to Islam are interconnected and this is a leading factor in the conversion to Islam.[66] The interfaith marriages in this study are not interracial, as observed in the Malaysian cases, but of the same ethnicity. Köse's research among seventy native British converts to Islam also revealed that "the relationship between the affectional motif and being married to a Muslim at the time of the conversion is significant."[67]

Lofland and Skonovd stated that, in the affectional motif, the potential convert has a strong liking or attachment for practicing members of the group.

---

63. Convert 1.
64. Convert 9.
65. Mohd Khambali, "Interfaith Marriage and Religious Conversion."
66. Mohd Khambali.
67. Köse, *Conversion to Islam*, 110.

The group or individual is perceived as caring, loving, and affirming, this is "social pressure but exists and functions more as 'support' and attraction than as 'inducement.'"[68] Applying this theory to the present study, it suggests that the requirement to convert to Islam before marriage is approved, serves as a social pressure because a woman cannot marry the man of their choice, if they don't convert. The scholarship awarded to some and the free gifts given may also be seen as social pressure and economic enticement, as well to win adherents to Islam. These Igbo converts in Mecca, Egypt, Saudi Arabia, etc., are studying Islam-related courses chosen for them before enrollment into those universities. They are also required to become Chief Imams in their various villages after graduation. This appears to lend support that this affection demonstrated toward Igbo converts is "social pressure but exists and functions more as 'support' and attraction than as 'inducement.'"[69]

One female convert converted only after marriage. Her husband did not compel her to convert, rather it was a personal decision due to her desire to have a religiously homogeneous and harmonious home. She reported,

> I had told my husband that I will not embrace that religion [Islam], that each person should go to his own religion. My husband consented and said I should continue with the Catholic [church] I was attending. So, I thought and asked myself a question, "when I give birth to a child, will this child follow my husband's religion or mine?" If I have a son and he says he will follow my husband, and a daughter she says she will follow me, this kind of thing divides a family. So, I said that it's good that I join my husband in his religion.[70]

The third motif is the mystical motif. Two (male) converts reported to have undergone a mystical experience before they embraced Islam. One participant reported seeing Jesus in a dream seated on a camel practicing Islam.

> It was Jesus Christ that was shown to me in my dream. I was in the dream in my corridor, I saw flowers everywhere and Jesus Christ was in the setting room performing *salat*. He was

---

68. Lofland and Skonovd, "Conversion Motifs," 380.
69. Lofland and Skonovd, 380.
70. Convert 19.

> performing *salat* [ablution] and reading the *tesibie* [prayer bead]. This *tesibie* he was reading was like the skin of a ram. So Jesus Christ showed me that he is not a Christian, but a Muslim. It was God who called me to join Islam.[71]

The second convert narrated a story of having seen Mohammad in his dream frowning at him for possessing a rosary and Catholic prayer book. This encounter did not compel him to convert, but after the death of his father, two elderly Muslim men passed by his house and enquired of the burial. Thereafter they exclaimed *allahukubari* three times and walked away. Immediately he decided to become a Muslim.

> I was just in front of my house and these two elderly men passed by my house and said "you are back, you are back. May God help me, may God help me, and may God help me." They finished this prayer and moved on. When they finished this prayer and moved on, I cannot explain again, I cannot explain anything to you again that happened, except that I went to an *onye Hausa*, his name is Mallam One. I told him that I want to enter Islam. We drove to TWO's home and he asked me if my father is a Muslim; I said, "no." "Is your mother a Muslim?" I said, "no." He asked me what I saw in Islam that influenced my decision. I said that it is because I want to enter Islam.[72]

Though only men reported this conversion type, the relationship between gender and mystical motif is not significant in this study. This appears to prove Lofland and Skonovd's assertion that "little or no social pressure is involved, rather the convert is even likely alone at the time of the actual event."[73] Both converts were alone at the time of the event and no social pressure was involved.

Next, we see the experimental motif, this motif was very rare in this study as just one interviewee reported to have experienced it. According to him, when he saw a messenger in the office with the Muslim prayer beads, he was curious and enquired about its meaning. The Muslim messenger patiently

---

71. Convert 15.
72. Convert 22.
73. Lofland and Skonovd, "Conversion Motifs," 377.

explained what the prayer beads were and how to us them. This interviewee wanted to give it a try, and today he is a committed Muslim.

Coercion was also present in this study. One convert alluded to his conversion as being coerced. The convert was a university student who shared a room with a Muslim friend. After they relocated to a mosque to be closer to the university, the friends of his roommate were pestering him to embrace Islam. He initially objected but, as they continued talking to him about it, he decided to embrace the religion.

> My roommate and I lived off campus, which was far from the university, so I began making plans to come down [closer] to school here to reduce expenses. So my friend told me that he is a Muslim, why not come down here [to the central mosque] so we can stay in the mosque and from the mosque, we can search for an apartment? So I consented, he said he is not forcing me to embrace his religion and we moved into the central mosque. Many of his Muslim brothers were forcing me to convert into Islam, I said, "no." So they were like trying to push me for roughly a month and then one day, I just decided to make up my mind and embraced the religion. So that is how I started.[74]

Gerlach and Hine discovered seven conversion stages a potential convert undergoes before conversion. The third model, known as re-education through group interaction, stipulates that, "to maintain and sustain commitment, the convert must identify with the values of the movement to grow through group interaction because commitment cannot be sustained in a vacuum. If external relationship is neutral or weak, the potential convert will quickly bond with the new religion."[75] This was present in the conversion of convert thirty above. His external relationship with Christians was neutral or weak because he had moved into the central mosque, and then his interaction was mostly with Muslims. He quickly bonded with this new religion though he was coerced.

---

74. Convert 30.
75. Gerlach and Hine, *People, Power, Change*, 113.

The revivalist motif: This motif was not brought up by any convert. However, there were two other reasons not covered by Lofland and Skonovd's theory that were discovered in this study – upward mobility and an adequate place to serve God and still marry. One convert stated that his conversion to Islam was as an opportunity to improve status. He stated that there are opportunities you may not have if you are not a Muslim. "The attraction for me is that, me also, I wanted to use that system also because I went to the north to learn work and it is because you are a Muslim that you can sit with somebody that is Muslim. If you are a Christian, you will not feel comfortable sitting with them."[76] Nnorom's research among the Igbo of Afikpo mentioned that the desire for greater status is a strategy Islam adopts in Igboland. This present study seems to concur with Nnorom's finding.

Looking for an adequate place to serve God and still marry was reported by one male convert as his conversion motif. He was a staunch Catholic, brought up by an Irish missionary, with the desire to become a Reverend Father, but his mother wanted him to bear children. In order to grant his mother's wish, he embraced Islam where he could serve as a minister and marry as well. Today, he is an Islamic preacher with a family.

> What influenced my decision in embracing Islam is because I wanted a way that I could serve my God and to be recognized as a Reverend Minister, which I did. I have my ID card because I belong to an organization known as the council of Ulama of Nigeria, I'm their field worker in KK. It was only self-conviction that took me to Islam, because I could not be in the reverendhood, and I need some other place where I can serve my God and to be recognized, then marry and bear children, issues like my mother told me.[77]

The conversion of the converts in this sample was gradual, it did not occur suddenly; rather a considerable number of months or years of study and reasoning were involved, often aided by Muslim friends. A significant number of the converts reported to have articulated their decision, considered

---

76. Convert 4.

77. Convert 17. Some place names have been altered for participant safety.

the advantages and disadvantages, and consciously studied the religion over time before embracing it.

The sudden and dramatic conversion types seem absent in this study, no convert reported these types in their conversion process. Their absence may be explained by the family background of the converts. The majority of these converts did not grow up in a committed Christian home or under a strong Christian influence. The majority of them grew up in a family where both parents practiced different religions, Christianity and Igbo tribal religion, or were of different denominations. For instance, one convert said, "they [the family members] were Catholics, my father was animist; it was my mother who was a Catholic,"[78] and another stated that "while I was attending a Catholic [church], my mother was attending CAC [Christ Apostolic Church]. My family was not attending the Catholic church; I was the only one attending a Catholic church."[79]

Sub-research Question 4: How Have They Changed as a Result of Their Conversion?

The converts described how their conversion to Islam changed their lives for good. It affected intellectual, moral, and social changes, including changes in beliefs and practices, behavior, social relations, loss of old friendships and family ties, as well as their relationships with the society in general.

Orji defines religious conversion as "a shift or movement into a new horizon."[80] This implies that the "converted comprehends differently, values differently, and also relates differently because one has effected a shift in one's horizon."[81] He further posits that conversion is not only an individual event but also multi-dimensional because it brings change on the intellectual, religious, social, and moral levels.

Intellectual conversion "helps to cast off false ideas and philosophies which one had imbibed for a very long time."[82] After the conversion of the converts in this study, they cast off the ideas and philosophies of their previous religion.

---

78. Convert 1.
79. Convert 16.
80. Orji, *Ethnic and Religious Conflicts*, 52.
81. Orji, 52.
82. Igboin, "Bias and Conversion," 169.

They all declared the Shahada, acknowledged the oneness of God, and Prophet Mohammad as his last messenger. They abandoned and rejected the Sonship of Jesus, his divinity, his mediatory role, the doctrine of the Trinity, and the doctrine of original sin.

They imbibed a new belief that Jesus was just a prophet, like any other prophet from Adam to Mohammad. They rejected that he died on the cross and accepted that he was only lifted to heaven. They currently believe that the mission of Jesus and Muhammad was the same. One convert stated that "God sent Moses to the Jews, Jesus to the Christians, and Mohammad to the Muslims with the same message."[83] They equate Jesus with Mohammad; "Jesus and the prophet Mohammad are both servants of the Most High God. Both of them are servants of God."[84] Further, they reported that Jesus predicted the coming of Mohammad in John 14:26: "But the Advocate, the Holy Spirit, whom the Father will send in my name, will teach you all things and will remind you of everything I have said to you."[85] According to them, this Scripture buttressed that no contention existed between Jesus and the Prophet Mohammad. The converts believe that the comforter Jesus spoke of here is Prophet Mohammad. One convert stated that, "the comforter is Muhammad because Muhammad is the last messenger."[86] In fact, these converts speak highly of Jesus and respect him in some cases better than Christians.

Conversion for them did not result to total renunciation of all Christian beliefs, rather their former Christian beliefs enabled them in understanding Islam. During the interview, they referred to the Bible in attempting to clarify the Qur'an's teaching on some issues. For instance one convert said,

> He [Jesus] asked them [Christians] to worship only one God. He said of myself I shall do nothing, as I hear I judge and my judgment is just. I seek not the will of myself but the will of the Father who sent me. Isn't it? That is what Jesus Christ said, you see he is not a God there. He is just like other prophets, you know, acting on instruction. In the book of Matthew, chapter 7:21, Jesus Christ rightly said that not everyone who says to me

---

83. Convert 2.
84. Convert 2.
85. Convert 30.
86. Convert 30.

Lord, Lord shall see the kingdom of heaven, but those that do the will of my father who is in heaven! What is Islam? Islam is to submit and surrender to the will of God.[87]

They claimed that Islam is fulfilling and it is of God because the Bible spoke of it. Therefore, they express no acrimony toward Christians or Christianity.

Religious conversion "is not simply a process of becoming, say a Christian or Muslim, but a total and radical re-orientation of one's life to God (not religion), that one surrenders, not only oneself, but also one's unadmitted deepest pretense to absolute personal autonomy."[88] The converts in this study re-oriented their lives to God by becoming intentional in their religious life and in their attempt to obey God. They stated that after their commitment to Islam, they began practicing the Islamic five times daily prayer and engaging in Ramadan. Some of them pray in Arabic, while most pray in the Igbo language. Those who pray in Arabic and read Qur'an in Arabic are those who attended Qur'an school and studied the religion after their conversion, at their own expense. One convert reported that the Hausa Muslims refused to teach him Arabic, so he sold all he had to acquire Islamic and Arabic knowledge.

> When I joined Islam, I became *almajiri*. *Almajiri* are those who beg alms for Islam, because I locked my shop, and sold my stove and pots in Kano to learn how to read the Qur'an in Arabic. [When] I was reading the Qur'an they [Hausa Muslims] said that I don't know how to read it and they didn't want to teach me how to read it. So, I sold everything I had and went to Jigawa state to study the Qur'an.[89]

The majority who pray in the Igbo language are those who did not have the opportunity to attend Qur'anic schools or study Islam but decided that their children will be exposed to the religion. One convert stated,

> It's just gradually, although I don't read Arabic; I did not have anybody to sponsor me to go deeper into Islam. It is just how to pray and the laws of Islam, don't do this, don't do that, that I know. That is why I said that these children [his children] will

---

87. Convert 2.
88. Orji, *Ethnic and Religious Conflicts*, 44.
89. Convert 22.

learn it. They are now attending Islamic school. They attend Qur'anic school every Saturday and Sunday, but when on vacation they attend it every day.[90]

The converts reported a significant change in their habits, like a turnaround from drinking, smoking and womanizing. One convert reported that "when they [his friends] saw my behavior, [they were amazed at the change] because when I was a Christian, I will not lie, I was a drunkard; I drank and smoked, but when I became a Muslim those things became taboo to me, I couldn't do them."[91]

Köse describes social conversion as such:

> the person who wants to remain converted must engineer his social life in accordance with his purpose. This may require the individual to disassociate himself from previous associates or groups that constituted the plausibility structure of his past religious reality, while he associates himself with those who sponsor him in his new religious reality.[92]

The converts in this study have disassociated themselves from their past religious reality and associated themselves to their new religious reality. However, their disassociation did not result in a radical termination of social roles and ties, though one convert did, as narrated above. Though the Igbo Christian converts are socially stigmatized, they still regard themselves as members of the *ummnna* (kinsmen), their community and society. They do not consider isolation an option, even when the society attempts to isolate them. Rather they endeavor to remain part of crucial social groups in their communities, retain their previous jobs, names (though they use their Islamic name within the Muslim community), and responsibilities. To them, there is no disparity between being Igbo and Muslim in their society. One convert narrates,

> We belong there [*ummunna* – kinsmen]. Among my family, I am the most senior, how can I leave them? The day my father died, I did all the ceremonial rites. They treat me differently, but I am enduring. We cannot leave our farm because it has been

---

90. Convert 12.
91. Convert 7.
92. Köse, *Conversion to Islam*, 139.

covered with bush. What is left for us is to weed the grasses, so we endure. There is a lot of endurance in terms of *umunna* problems.[93]

These converts remained part and parcel of their society, age grades, and *umunna* but avoid participation in any activity that contradicts their new faith, or makes a financial contribution toward anything that is haram. One convert radically disassociated himself from his kindred and community and any social involvement.

> I don't have a problem with anybody and do not belong to any group meeting [fellow kinsmen, kindred like *umunna*]; I go my way and they go theirs. I don't belong to any group in the land. I am on my own and they [kinsmen] are on their own. There is nothing we do together; when I die they should not come to bury me. Go your way; is there any problem with that?[94]

Moral conversion "is a matter of deciding to act responsibly and inculcating a value-laden ethics in which one is governed by the criterion of what is truly good as against apparent good that merely satisfies one's immediate demands for self-gratification."[95] After conversion, the converts in this sample began acting responsibly and ethically by their change of habits and practices (avoiding alcoholic drink, eating pork, un-halal food, partying, etc.). For some, this change was immediately after conversion, while there are others who still kept some of their past habits but are gradually dropping them.

> I used to drink and smoke when I was a Christian but when I became a Muslim those things became taboo to me. I couldn't do it because on my day of baptism [induction into Islam] that was the first warning I was given that If I am in alcohol I should stop. And really, I drank it and attended the prayer, it did not suit me because it looks like something I am hiding from my people and you cannot hide such a thing. No matter how you hide, they will still understand that you are into such, so I have to stop it.[96]

---

93. Convert 17.
94. Convert 29.
95. Orji, *Ethnic and Religious Conflicts*, 55.
96. Convert 7.

So, for some their moral change was immediate, while for others it was gradual. This portrays that change of old practices or habits does not occur instantaneously, but progressively.

There was very little observable change in the new converts' dress codes; many retained their dress codes. Of the twenty-seven males interviewed, four wear Islamic attire, the long flowing robe and turban. While one female out of seven interviewed wears a veil. The male interviewees who did not adopt an Islamic dress code reported that Islam does not teach on dressing like a particular tribe. For instance, one convert stated, "You can see my attire [he dressed in trousers and a shirt], are you getting me? Islam doesn't tell you to wear Hausa clothes or dress in a particular way, but Islam directed you how you can wear your clothes."[97] Two female participants stated the Islamic law is binding on women to wear a hijab and stated that they do not leave their homes with their heads unveiled. Surprisingly, both of them were not wearing Islamic attire and while moving to another family they neither changed their attire nor wore a veil. So, on the issue of dress code, the majority of Igbo converts in this sample retained their dress code, while a few did not. This seems to concur with Okorocha's assertion that the Igbo rejected Islam in the past because Islam was presented to the Igbo with lots of required cultural attire, which the Igbo considered as unprogressive. Though some of the Igbo are accepting Islam, the majority of converts appear to be reluctant in adopting the Muslim dress code because the dress code is associated to Hausa culture, and they do not want to be associated with the Hausa. However, there are a few who have adopted the Muslim dress code.

The Igbo converts to Islam stated that their lives changed drastically after their conversion to Islam. The changes included: avoidance of alcoholic drinks; peace of mind and contentment; praying regularly; understanding that Allah is the creator; better treatment of others; one is now an Islamic preacher; changes in behavior; physical healing; material blessings; provision for basic needs of the converts and their families; as well as securing scholarship to study abroad.

> Well, *allamdurulai*, it has shaped my life. Well, I thank God; I give God the glory because there are lots of changes. The fact

---

97. Convert 6.

that, ever since I embraced Islam, I think the word I can use is peace, I found peace within myself, yeah.[98]

The knowledge of Islam has changed so many things in my life. It has taught me how to control my desire! [emphasized this desire], and it has brought contentment into my life. Above all it has made me to know that whatever happens to me is by Allah's design. So, I should not blame anybody, rather I blame myself. In fact, Islam has made me to be happy with myself and, at the same time, at peace with my neighbors.[99]

But when they see my behavior, because when I was a Christian, I will not lie, I was a drunkard. I drank and smoke, but when I became a Muslim, those things became taboo to me; I couldn't do it. In my village, people are now baffled to see me, saying I don't drink again, I don't smoke again, and they watch me all through the day and they don't see me drinking. When they bring drinks, I will say I am not taking part. There are many things they will bring that I will not take part. So, they get surprised, this man! I am very sorry, even in Port-Harcourt, some of my friends, when I stopped drinking, they said if this one can stop drinking, then I too can stop drinking.[100]

As has been observed in this section, the converts in this study changed significantly after their conversions to Islam. This change included change in religious practices and beliefs, relationships, worldview, and habits. A few changed their dress code, while majority retained their previous code of dressing. Their changes are ongoing, but they have social ties with family members, community and kindred. Their relationship with their communities is not severed, although defined because the converts choose what aspect of the relationship requirement to reject or accept.

---

98. Convert 20.
99. Convert 25.
100. Convert 7.

Other Emerging Themes

The data revealed some other themes which were not envisaged or included in the research questions. I shall discuss these themes in this section.

Igbo Christians' Response to Igbo Muslims' Theological Objections

When Igbo converts to Islam pose questions or challenge the Igbo Christians on the issues of the Sonship of Jesus or other theologically contentious topics between both religious faiths, the Christians display ignorance and show themselves ill-equipped to respond to such theological challenges. This brings them down before the same Muslims they seek to evangelize. One convert reported,

> I asked them, where did Jesus tell you people that he is God? I told them to give me a quotation where Jesus said that he is God. They could not show me. Another pastor came to witness to me and I asked him, do you know why Muslims wash their legs and hands before prayer? Do you not know where it is in the Bible? I told him to go and check it, he did not even know that such a thing is in the Bible until that day. He could not say anything and left.[101]

This finding indicates that the converts begin studying the Bible in addition to the Qu'ran after conversion. This enables them to distort the truth in the Bible to fit into their arguments from the Qu'ran. These converts are also trained by older Muslims on how to respond to Christian objection to the Qu'ran as well as lifting a passage from the Bible to support Islamic teaching. This skill and training are absent in Christianity in Igbo society.

Igbo Muslims' Position on Jihad

The majority of converts in this study oppose the issue of killing in the name of Allah; they interpret that part of Qur'an quite differently. In fact, they claimed that such teaching is not in the Qu'ran, it is a lack of knowledge, as well as ignorance on the part of those who embark on such improper misinterpretation of the Qur'an. The following are a few cases to illustrate

---

101. Convert 18.

this. One convert stated, "No! no! it's not good. No, it is not normal. I have never read about that in the Scripture, and I have not seen it. So, if any set of people is doing it, they are doing it because it is their tradition."[102] Another posited: "No good Muslim can take a knife and kill you; he cannot tell you a lie, let alone kill. He prays five times a day, where does he want those five daily prayers to go? That prayer cannot be answered; it cannot allow you to do that."[103] Yet another said,

> When people come today [and] they claim that Islam gave you sword to kill people, and you will go to heaven, it's a lie! It's a lie. As I have earlier said that God said "beware of the blood of my creation." That means you must never kill. But when you see the Hausa man killing, they are doing their politics. The Hausa man is interested in power and he is ready to kill you if you are not Hausa, he is ready![104]

This shows that the Igbo Christian converts to Islam are not open to killing fellow Igbo in the name of religion. Also, they have a different interpretation from the Hausa Muslims on the issue of jihad. However, the Hausa Muslims love and promote any Igbo man who antagonizes a non-Igbo Muslim. One male convert stated,

> You see, the Hausa man loves any Igbo that will go and kill his mother and bring her to them. They are ready to give you millions to kill your mother and bring her to them! Because what they love is anybody that will be antagonistic to his people, Igbo! A Hausa man will promote him because he is the one that does not care about his people, and is ready to destroy his people.[105]

Igbo Converts' Justification of Their Conversion

The Igbo converts to Islam justified their conversion as an exercise of their franchise to choose any religion they so wish. Many of them quoted the Qur'an, "There is no compulsion in religion" to support their conversion.

---

102. Convert 30.
103. Convert 21.
104. Convert 16.
105. Convert 16.

Most importantly, they claimed to be adults and, as adults, no one can dictate to them what to accept or reject.

> As I have my freedom to choose where to worship my creator, so every other person has his or hers, but it's not something that should bring acrimony. I have the right to choose where I want to belong because religion is something of the heart, it is a personal thing.[106]

> So actually, there is no compulsion in Islam and, when you are an adult, you have the right to choose whichever religion that is of your interest.[107]

> the truth there is that, I think, when it comes to religion, it's a matter of choice. You don't force someone into a religion. So, I think I've chosen the right path and I want to be on the right path.[108]

> They [his family] did nothing, they have no option, they can't dictate to me, I am a matured man. They cannot dictate to me; there is a stage you yourself will reach [when] you cannot dictate for your children.[109]

This finding indicates that the Igbo Christian converts to Islam differ significantly from the Hausa Muslims on this issue. There is no justification for a Hausa person to convert to Christianity; the person has no right to do that though the Qur'an states that there is no compulsion in religion yet, it is apostasy to do so. This finding equally lends credence to Victor Uchendu's assertion that the Igbo are individualistic in nature and are open to change.[110]

Existing Relationship between Muslim-Christian Spouses and Their Children

The data revealed two kinds of relationships that exist between husbands, wives, and the children with both religious faiths in the home. Those males

---

106. Convert 2.
107. Convert 6.
108. Convert 19.
109. Convert 3.
110. Uchendu, *Igbo of Southeast Nigeria*.

who converted to Islam after marriage and childbearing have cordial relationships with family. The married male converts claimed that they cannot compel their wives or children to embrace Islam; though they desire and hope they would embrace Islam. One convert reported thus:

> They [his wife and children] are not all Muslims; that is the challenge I was telling you about, they are all grown up. I will not compel them to become Muslims but, by the wish of God, *insha Allah*, if God wants them to become Muslims I think one or two can follow my line. But at the moment, I cannot be fighting with them because they are not Muslims.[111]

Those whose wives embraced the religion with them after marriage, along with their children, expect their daughters to marry Muslims. However, these men are open to giving their daughters in marriage to a Christian, in order to avoid shame of having their daughters impregnated. Some considered themselves broad-minded, claiming that love is paramount in marriage not religion, therefore, approved of the marriage of their daughters with a non-Muslim man. The following two case studies below attest to this:

> My other daughter is married with seven children; she is married to a pastor! I am a broad-minded man. It's not alright to impose your choice on your children. Suppose they say, "I love this man," and you say, "No, he is a Christian." Then they elope with him or get pregnant by him; it's a shame to you. So better to allow them.[112]

> my children are Muslims, but others married Christians, except one, because the Holy Book commands that you should not allow your child to get pregnant before marriage.[113]

> I will not approve my daughter to marry a Christian. But, if she insists that it must be this person, you cannot kill her. She will go, but for me, I won't like it, simple.[114]

---

111. Convert 7.
112. Convert 21.
113. Convert 18.
114. Convert 11.

The second kind of relationship that exists is that of tension, anger, and pain. This is observed among male convert who married a Christian wife after conversion because of lack of Muslim Igbo women to marry. Such relationships are characterized by tension and anger, especially when the Christian wife refuses to convert to Islam. One male convert narrated how he ended up marrying a Christian wife after a fruitless search for an Igbo Muslim woman. He had hoped that she would convert after marriage, but that has been impossible. He punished her, and even stopped her from attending church for over a year, and yet she still maintains her faith. He even thought of divorcing her, but his Igbo Muslim brothers advised against it, encouraging him not to take the law into his own hands.

> I travelled everywhere searching for an Igbo Muslim wife when I saw that all of my juniors were getting married, even some have great grandsons. So, I looked into it. It was too much a thing, so I just went to who was available to me, hoping that she will change. But since that time, I have tried my possible best to change her, but it's not working. It is one of the biggest problems I have now. It is annoying me so, I don't want to know where she worships. I am not happy with it. Even when I attend my Muslim meetings, they say to me that God has the right to do things. Though I get to a point that I want to boycott [divorce] her since she cannot change, but they told me that I am taking the law into my [own] hands and not respecting the law of Islam; that is not the right thing to do. So, I should leave it. Tomorrow she may change; any time she may change. She is a Christian, even though for some time I stopped her from going to church, but of recent she started going again. She stopped for almost a year, but of recent she has started going.[115]

In the above cases, the relationships between the spouses are not cordial. His anger and annoyance are compounded because of some opportunities and benefits that bypass him because his wife is a non-Muslim. He stated that when the wives of the Igbo Muslims are invited to the government house in his state, Ebonyi State, she does not attend because she is a non-Muslim.

---

115. Convert 27.

Thus, all the gifts distributed to the Muslim wives elude him and this hurts him deeply.

CHAPTER 5

Discussion, Conclusion and Recommendations

Introduction

One fundamental question that prompted this study was "what are the reasons Igbo Christians give for their conversion to Islam?" To achieve this purpose, the qualitative research method was adopted. The investigation was conducted in various parts of Igboland, including: Nssukka, Enugu, Okija, Owerri, Afikpo, Obollo Afor, and Igbagwa, where the converts either hailed from or reside. The investigation was conducted over about six months within a three-year time period. In 2014, I visited one field site (Afikpo) to survey the place and do a pilot test. In 2015, I spent three months visiting and interviewing converts in the above-mentioned Igbo regions, except Okija. While in 2017, I traveled again to all these regions, including Okija, for more in-depth contact with the converts. I left the field at the point of saturation, I discovered that I was not getting any new stories from what I already had.

Thirty Igbo converts to Islam were purposefully selected and contacted through the Chief Imams, Muslims, missionaries, pastors, and other referrals. An in-depth, face-to-face ethnographic interview and observation were adopted to elicit information from the converts. A tape-recorder, with permission of the converts, was used to record the information. The interviews were conducted in the central mosques, shops and homes of the converts, as preferred by the converts.

The data was collected using a Microsoft word processing program. Upon the completion of data collection, I transferred all data from the tape-recorder to two other devices: a laptop and an external drive. Second, I transcribed all the data myself; this enabled me to master the data, internalize it, and observe any emerging themes. I transcribed the interviews verbatim as recorded, including coughs, laughs, sighs, pauses, telephone rings, and other interruptions, as recorded on the tapes.

Third, I read and studied the transcribed texts keenly to observe any emerging themes and patterns. I did this with an open attitude, seeking what emerges as important and of interest from the texts. Fourth, I made a working copy of all the transcripts. This copy I worked with, making reference to the original copy as need arose. I reread and studied again this working copy of the transcripts, marking and labeling passages of interest. This process is called coding. Finally, I created several categories and organized (coded) the excerpts in these categories. I copied and filed the coded texts that fit into the created categories. After filing all the coded texts into the categories, I reread all of them file by file, sifting out the ones that appeared very compelling and which answered the research questions. I sat aside those texts not related to the research questions. However, I discovered interesting themes from them later that my research never sought to discover. After the completion of coding, categorizing, filing and documenting, I moved to interpret the data by answering the research questions, discussing emerging themes, examining the applicability of theories discussed in chapter 2 and other previous studies.

Summary of the Findings

For the research thirty Igbo Christian converts to Islam were interviewed, twenty-three males and seven females. They originated from and resided in various parts of Igboland. The majority of the converts were educated; very few had little or no education. This shows that conversion to Islam in Igboland occurs among people with varying educational backgrounds. It further reveals that religious conversion is not dependent upon educational qualifications; a PhD holder can change to a totally different religious faith the same as someone who has no secondary education. This might amaze others, it appears to be more of the matter of heart, conviction, and rationality.

The converts were gainfully employed and engaged occupationally, thus had sources of livelihood. Therefore, their conversion was not influenced by desire for material gain or job opportunities. Most of them were already married with families of their own prior to conversion, though nine converted because of opportunities perceived in Islam, such as marriage (common among women), education, and kindness of Muslims.

Some of the converts came from families where both parents were practicing dual religion (Christianity and African Traditional Religion), same religion (ATR), dual denomination (Catholic and Christ Apostolic church, Anglican and Catholic), and some attending the same denomination. Some of their families were marked with tension and anger, especially those from polygamous families. From my data, most of them came from families where the parents were not committed Christians, so, they were not fully socialized to being Christians. However, a good number of them along the way became committed Christians, though their families were not very religious. However, all the converts described themselves as Christians prior to conversion, though their level of commitment to the religion differed.

Of the converts studied, fourteen considered themselves as weak and nominal while in Christianity and three converts considered themselves young prior to their conversion. Religion for them was merely something called Christianity, Islam or Hinduism. For this category, conversion means a transformation, "taking of a new way of life in place of the old . . . a deliberate turning from indifference, a turning which implies a consciousness that a great change is involved, that the old was wrong and the new is right."[1] Transformation occurs in two ways, either turning to piety within the religion to which one adheres or exchanging the beliefs or practices of their religion for another. For these Igbo converts, transformation did not occur within Christianity, but in a different religion – Islam. This seems to indicate that they believed that transformation can occur in other religions, but not in Christianity.

Thirteen converts considered themselves committed Christians while in Christianity. They had a clear understanding of the evangelistic perception of what it is to be a Christian. Some had even accepted Jesus Christ as their Lord and Savior, attended church regularly (including weekly services), were

---

1. Nock, *Conversion*, 7.

baptized (infant baptism), received the Eucharist, engaged in the activities of the church, contributed to the projects of the church, belonged to one or two groups in the church, taught catechism, or were trained to become a Reverend Father. These converts (except two males) became disenchanted and disillusioned and changed to Islam. Their disillusionment was not with the theological beliefs or practices of Christianity, but with the attitudes and behaviors of some Christians and pastors. For these Igbo converts, conversion meant and means transformation – exchanging their Christian beliefs and practices to another religion (Islam). They carried over the same dedication, commitment, and adherence they exhibited in Christianity to Islam. They observe and obey Qur'anic teachings, observe the Ramadan, engage in *da'wah*, serve as Chief Imams, and pray regularly. Thus, their conversion seems to be a carry-over of their commitment from Christianity to Islam. The only change is exchange of beliefs and practices to a different religion.

Each of the converts underwent six stages in their conversion process. Six of seven conversion stages in the model proposed by Gerlach and Hine were involved in the converts conversion process. First, they had initial contact with a practicing Muslim, like a neighbor, friend, husband, family member, or a colleague. In the second stage, they observed positive change, fulfillment, and seriousness with the things of God in the life of their friends, relatives, colleagues, or neighbors who are Muslims. Third, these converts were re-educated via preaching; teaching of Islamic values, ideology, beliefs, practices, and prayers; explanations; and provision of Islamic materials to read from their Muslim friends. By the end of this stage, the Igbo converts reached the fourth stage of making decisions to surrender their old identities (Christians) and embrace new identities. The fifth stage was an event to mark their commitment to their new religion. This event was the confession of faith, like taking of Shahada pronounced before a crowd of witnesses that "there is no god but God and Mohammad is his messenger." The last stage involved experiencing the consequences of their conversion. These converts faced rejection, isolation, ridicule, threats, insults, name calling, hatred, attempted murder, abandonment, dissolution of marriage, enmity, and anger from their families and the society around them. Despite these negative consequences, they have remained Muslims and some have vowed to die Muslims. Their various reasons given for conversion were seven:

Discussion, Conclusion and Recommendations

1. Intellectual: Islam is more rational and logical.
2. Affectional: The opportunities for care, material assistance, and marriage, but these are "social pressure but exists and functions as support."[2] Marriage played a vital role at times because for Igbo Christian women to marry an Igbo Muslim man, she had to convert to Islam, though two male converts' wives did not.
3. Mystical: dream and divine encounters.
4. Experimental: giving practicing Islam a try and in the process embracing it.
5. Coercion: force, pressure, or mind control.
6. Upward mobility.
7. Acceptable religion to become minister of God as well as having a family.

However, the two most motivating reasons were intellectual and affectional.

Lastly, the converts became transformed after their conversions. Seventeen, who considered themselves nominal, weak, and young while in Christianity, have taken religion seriously now, changing their lifestyles and living differently as Muslims. The thirteen who were already transformed while in Christianity, but disenchanted and disillusioned with the attitudes of some Christians and pastors, changed their allegiance to Islam, exchanging their beliefs, practices and commitment to Islam.

Discussion

This study set out to identify the reasons the Igbo Christian converts to Islam give for their conversions. The findings of this work have shown the following in the order of the research question and sub-research questions:

First, conversion among the Igbo Christians occurred irrespective of gender, age, profession, family background, social and religious background, occupation, marital status, or exposure. Converts originated from polygamous families, different religious affiliations, different denominations or attended the same denomination. Despite emerging from families that were animistic and did not take religion seriously, thirteen of the converts became committed

---

2. Lofland and Skonvod, "Conversion Motifs," 380.

Christians along the way while seventeen were nominal Christians. This indicates that a person can deviate from the original religion of their family as they get older. One would have assumed that having grown up in an animistic family, the converts would remain animists, or having grown up in a relatively Christian family, one would remain a Christian. This study shows that people do not always retain the religion of their parents.

It is interesting to note that the seventeen converts that considered themselves weak and nominal while Christians became transformed when they converted to Islam and took religion seriously, while the thirteen converts that considered themselves committed Christians also became committed Muslims. It seems absurd for a Christian who once accepted Jesus Christ as Lord and Savior and was committed to the things of a Christian God to gradually reject, and deny them all, in exchange for a totally different religion that has different views of God. This research has shown that a human being is susceptible to religious change, despite how rooted or committed they may have been in their previous religion. On the other hand, it also shows that conversion can occur in any religion. This is observed in the transformation of seventeen nominal Christians, who are now Muslims.

Second, this study demonstrates that converts changing to a different religion pass through stages. The converts in this study went through six stages, rather than seven as proposed by some scholars. Varying numbers of converts passed through a different number of the stages, but all of them went through three of the stages: decision and surrender, commitment event, and consequences. This indicates that there are certain stages of conversion that every potential convert must undergo in their conversion journey.

Third, the main finding of this study is that there exist seven reasons that influenced Igbo Christians to embrace Islam: intellectual, affectional, mystical, experimental, coercive, upward mobility, and as suitable to serve God and get married.

The most motivating reasons given for conversion were intellectual. This means that the converts read Islamic books and materials, and listened to lectures, concluding in the end that Islam is more logical and rational than Christianity. It is popularly claimed by Nigerian Christians that the Igbo convert to Islam primarily due to material/financial benefits. The literature indicates that the Igbo converted to Christianity from Igbo primal religion due to the opportunities and benefits Christianity provided them. However, this appears absent in the conversion of this study's Igbo in this category. These findings reveal that many Igbo Christians are reading Islamic materials and listening to Islamic lectures as well. This appears unnoticed in Igboland, but it is quietly going on.

Another dominant reason given for Igbo converting to Islam is affectional. Muslims are perceived as loving, caring, and affirming, nine converts embraced Islam for this reason. Four males embraced Islam because of the Muslims' kindness and love for one another, depicted in their helping others, awarding of scholarships, and being serious with the things of God. The five females embraced Islam in order to marry their Muslim spouses. As Islam requires, to marry a Muslim the non-Muslim must convert to Islam. Here, the marriage serves as social pressure, the scholarship awarded to some Igbo to study abroad, as well as Muslims' kindnesses have served as social pressure, though these function as support. The women may not have been as likely to have converted to Islam if it was not required for their marriage to be approved. Also, one male convert converted to Islam due to the opportunity it offered him to improve his status quo.

We may also conclude that conversion for material benefit is present in this example (six converts), but mostly among women, due to a desire to be married to a Muslim. All of these examples indicate that the most effective strategies for conversion to Islam in Igboland is intellectual among both males and females (ten males and six females), and affectional (five females and four men) especially marriage being applicable to many females under the affectional motif.

Fourth, this study equally demonstrates that observable positive changes occurred in the converts' lives after conversion. The converts in this study claim to have abandoned their old "bad" way of living and adopted new lifestyles, worldviews, habits, and attitudes. The changes in some of their lives are obvious enough to the extent that some other villagers want to embrace the religion as well.

An Examination of the Findings in Relation to Existing Research

My findings both refute and confirm earlier studies regarding religious conversion. My findings are broadly consistent with other studies on the backgrounds and motifs of Christian conversion to Islam. For example, looking at the works of Köse, Dikki, and Kim, they all (including the present study) reveal that most of the Christian converts to Islam are educated and apparently successful in their fields of work prior to their conversion to Islam. Also their first contact with Islam was mostly through close personal contact with Muslims who provided Islamic materials for them, had discussions about Islam, and answered questions or objections about Islam. The intellectual and affectional motifs were the most motivating factors for conversion. Additionally, the conversions occur throughout various Christian denominations, but with the highest numbers coming from the particular denomination of Roman Catholicism.

The similar study conducted in Kenya revealed that six converts were Pentecostals, four Catholics, and one Presbyterian.[3] In a British case, fifty-one were from the Church of England (known as Anglican Church in Africa), twelve Catholics, four Jews, and three Methodist.[4] In a South Korean case, Protestants were sixteen, Catholics two, Buddhism one, Confucianism one, and no religious affiliation six.[5] In this Nigerian case, twenty-two converts were from a Catholic background, four from the Anglican Church of Nigeria, three Pentecostal, and one Presbyterian. This is one of the areas where my study differs from previous studies. Though they had some converts to Islam from Catholicism in their studies, the numbers of Catholics in my case outweighs theirs.

My finding that conversion to Islam among most women is interconnected with marriage concurs with Mohd Khambali.[6] The interfaith marriage in this study is not interracial, as observed in the Malaysian case, but within the same ethnicity. Köse's research also revealed that "the relationship between the affectional motif and being married to a Muslim at the time of the conversion is significant."[7] This is confirmed by my study, where five women's conversions to Islam were related to marriage.

---

3. Dikki, "Missiological Study of Islamic Strategies."
4. Köse, *Conversion to Islam*, 196.
5. Kim and Mehmedoglu, "Conversion Motifs."
6. Mohd Khambali, "Interfaith Marriage."
7. Köse, *Conversion to Islam*, 110.

Uchendu, in her book, enumerated several reasons for Igbo conversion to Islam, which my findings give credence to as well. However, my work differs in the organization of these reasons. Mine are organized in light of Lofland and Skonovd's conversion theory, which enabled me to classify them into categories with the number of converts under each category. At a glance, one can more easily observe the most motivating motif for Igbo conversion to Islam in this study.

My findings also give credence to Ottenberg's assertion from the literature review as well. He asserted that the Igbo are "probably most receptive to culture change, and most willing to accept Western ways, of any large group in Nigeria . . . Igbo could become all this without himself being changed significantly deep down inside."[8] The Igbo willingness to accept the Arab religion illustrates his point as well. The converts in this study accept certain aspects of the religion and reject others; some chose to retain their dress code and they have been given an Islamic name, but retain their Igbo names. For example, a convert could bear the name Ibrahim Chinedu or Aisha Ebere. Some of the Igbo Chief Imams preach using the Igbo language in the mosque and present Islam in the Igbo language on television and radio, rather than requiring converts to learn the Arabic holy language. Their explanation of certain issues in the Qur'an differs from the Hausa Muslims as well, such as their explanation of jihad differs significantly.

However, contrary to Ottenberg's claims covered in the literature review, my findings showed that most of the converts did change significantly deep down inside. The changes can be observed in their new allegiance, obedience to the Qur'an, and in changed behaviors and attitudes. However, their changes did not include a change of identity as an Igbo; they still consider themselves Igbo first, then Muslim.

My findings are contrary to Okoracha's position in the literature that the Igbo's goal of religion is salvation, understood as viable life, better life, and higher social status. He argues that the Igbo quickly accept any system or religion that provides this salvation. This research reveals that a good number of the converts did not convert to Islam for viable life, though some did. Five females converted in order to get married, one man for a felt need of upward mobility, and another man because of some of the promises Islam offered.

---

8. Ottenberg, "Ibo Receptivity to Change," 130, 216.

This later motivation for conversion is similar with one of Carol Virginia McKinney's findings in her research among the Bajju of Central Nigeria.[9] She discovered that one of the motivations for Bajjus conversion to Christianity was the opportunities for education and advancement offered by missions and churches. Though she focused on conversion from traditional religion to Christianity, it appears that some of the factors for conversion into any religion are the same, such as this one for material benefits or a perceived better lifestyle.

As Rambo postulated, these findings confirm that conversion is a gradual process, not sudden.[10] The converts in this study became involved in a prolonged gradual process that consisted of conversing with Muslims, reading Islamic literature, observing the lifestyle of Muslims, and attending Islamic lectures in the mosques, before deciding to convert.

Yang and Abel developed a model of seven stages an individual must pass through for conversion to occur. The first three are termed "predisposing conditions," this is when people turn to religion for lack of something, absolute deprivation, poverty or bad health. While the last four are termed "situational contingencies," which can be encountering a member of the other religion, having a pre-existent bond with a convert in the other religion, having a neutral relationship or experiencing a break in attachment to relationships in their old religion, or exposure to intensive interaction with the new religion. The majority of the converts in this study had no predisposing condition, they experienced no spiritual distress or crisis. They were neither deprived nor in abject poverty, though one convert had a prolonged illness that drove him to seek help from a Muslim. Though any predisposing conditions were unobvious in these findings, situational contingencies, on the other hand, were obvious. This supports Lofland and Stark's claim in chapter 2 that complete conversion will not occur without the situational contingencies, despite how predisposed the seeker may be.[11]

Furthermore, the findings are broadly consistent with the Muslim understanding of conversion, as defined by Muslim scholars in the literature. Murad stated that "coming to Islam is like going back to one's own roots in nature

---

9. McKinney, "Bajju of Central Nigeria," 12.
10. Rambo, *Understanding Religious Conversion*.
11. Lofland and Stark, "Becoming a World Saver," 865–875.

and history."[12] The Igbo converts claimed that they were only returning to their original religion, because everyone is born a Muslim but the family the child was born into brought the child up in a different religion. One convert, for example, stated that it was the parents who chose Christianity for him. The converts return to Islam involved the declaration of Shahada, induction, change of name (and attire in only few cases), and an ongoing observation of Islamic teachings. This is similar to what is found in Islamic literature.

Similarly, these findings concur with the work of Hamilton, cited by J. Dudley Woodberry, that converts' change to Islam is at three various levels.[13] The Igbo converts in this study are at the first and second levels, total conversion. Some have accepted inwardly the spirit and principles of Islam (level 1), while others have accepted the outward duties but not the spirit (level 2).

The observable changes after conversion that Lonergan and Orji discussed were supported by the findings of this study as well. They are intellectual, religious, moral, and affective changes in the lives of converts, as previously noted in chapter 4.

Additionally, the findings concur with anthropologists' understanding of conversion, especially as defined by Buckser and Glazier. They asserted that religious conversion involves changing one's religion and "to change one's religion is to change one's world, to voluntarily shift the basic presuppositions upon which both self and others are understood."[14] They further argued that "conversion is usually an individual process, involving a change of worldview and affiliation by a single person, but it occurs within a context of institutional procedures and social relationship."[15] This individual process was confirmed by the Igbo converts' change to Islam in this study.

Historians have described religious conversion in three ways: acculturation, adhesion/hybridity and syncretism, and transformation/turn to piety.[16] The Igbo conversions to Islam in this study fall into the third meaning – transformation, which indicates that my findings lend additional credence to

---

12. Murad, *Da'wah among Non-Muslims*, 16.
13. Woodberry, *Conversion in Islam*, 25.
14. Buckser and Glazier, *Anthropology of Religious Conversion*, xi.
15. Buckser and Glazier, xi.
16. Baer, *Honored by the Glory of Islam*.

historians' understanding of conversion. I am only using the Igbo conversions in this study to confirm or refute findings of previous studies.

Similarly, the current research also lends some credence to psychologists' assertions that negative psychological conditions precede conversion.[17] However, this was present in the narrative experience of only three male converts of this study. Thus, psychologists' claims may not be as generalized or universal. Last, but not the least, my findings confirm that the conversion phenomenon is indeed a complex one, and no single discipline can adequately explain it.

Highlights of Interesting, New or Unexpected Findings Discovered

In the course of this study, I discovered certain interesting and unexpected issues. For instance, I discovered that persecution for abandonment of one's religion of origin is not limited to Islam. The converts in this study were persecuted severely by family members for abdicating Christianity. Interestingly, they endured and still endure the persecution while remaining Muslims.

Second, before embarking on the study, I was concerned about accessing the converts because I assumed they would be hostile. This is due to the hostile relationship that exists between Christians and Muslims in Nigeria, as well as against the Boko Haram insurgents.[18]

Non-Igbo Muslims often accuse the Igbo Muslims of associating with *ndi Hausa* (the Hausa of Northern Nigeria) and calling them Boko Haram. Surprisingly, the converts were welcoming, accepting, approachable, and divulged information freely. They were quite excited to see an Igbo Christian interested in hearing their stories. One convert stated that "many people have been coming here from universities to interview me about tradition, Obollo tradition, and how it began. They even come from Delta, but I have not seen those who come to ask about the church and Muslims, I have not seen it, this is first time."[19] These Igbo Muslim converts were just like every other

---

17. Paloutzian, "Psychology of Religious Conversion."

18. Boko Haram is a terrorist organization in Nigeria, founded in 2002, with an ideology of fundamentalism influenced by *wahhabisim*, they advocate for a strict form of sharia law and oppose Western education. Wikipedia, "Boko Haram."

19. Convert 29.

Igbo person I know. I sat with the men in the mosques with uncovered hair, non-Islamic attire, talking in the Igbo language, cracking jokes and laughing. They called other Igbo Muslim converts to be interviewed, connected me to others via phone calls, and even took me to their shops and homes for interviews. I least expected this kind of hospitable treatment. I realized that Igbo Muslims and converts are different from the Hausa Muslims. In Northern Nigeria, the scenario would have been quite the opposite. This indicates that conversion, to Igbo Muslim converts, does not mean antagonizing fellow Igbo and rejecting the Igbo way of life, though two converts were a little more extreme in this behavior.

Though Boko Haram ideology and practice is absent among many Igbo Muslim converts in this study, this could be because Islam in Igboland is still in an early orthodox stage. This might change when it gets to the reform stage, if Islam gains many Igbo adherents. This could be a point of future research if Islam does overtake Christianity among the Igbo eventually.

Furthermore, I had thought that my gender (female) would hamper or limit my ability to interview men. On the contrary, it did not; many men availed themselves, accepted me and granted me an interview with them. The Hausa Muslim concept of Islam, that women are prohibited to sit and interact with men, was not observed in my case. Their conversion to Islam did not appear to affect this aspect of their Igbo cultural behavior toward women, me specifically.

This finding is in sharp contrast with Nnorom's, where he argued that the Islamization of Igbo poses a danger to Igbo interests and survival.[20] In fact, he lamented that "*Ndigbo no na nsegbu* [The Igbo are in trouble]."[21] On the contrary, my findings show that the Igbo Muslims interviewed are peaceful and live harmoniously with their non-Muslim family members, despite the rejection and ill treatment meted on them by their families. However, Ottenberg's research showed that conversion of the Anohia to Islam brought dissension between them and their neighboring town Kpogrikpo. These two Igbo communities lived harmoniously prior to Anohia's acceptance of Islam; the harmony was destroyed after Anohia's conversion to Islam. Possibly both our findings are accurate and would indicate that two sets of Igbo Muslims

---

20. Nnorom, "Islam in Igboland," 1.
21. Nnorom, 1.

exist in Igboland: the peaceful and non-peaceful adherents. This further supports my theory that if the number of Muslims in Igboland increases to a majority, they could be less hospitable to Igbo Christians.

It was surprising to discover from my research that Igbo Christians' motives for conversion are not totally different from other types of conversions (traditional to Christian or traditional to Islam, for example), people convert to other religions for similar reasons and report similar transformations. The transformation of these Igbo converts after their conversion to Islam, challenged my previous thoughts that transformation only occurs in Christianity. Conversion for these converts was not just accepting the oneness of Allah through the confession of Shahada, but they also reported a change in their attitudes and behavior. The observed difference between their conversion and Christian conversion is that Christians confess Christ and accept him as personal Lord and Savior, but the expected and observable changes in a true Christian convert were observed in these Muslim converts as well.

Contributions or Practical Applications of the Study

The findings of this study contribute to the service of the following sets of organizations, scholarship, and individuals:

Scholarship

My findings contribute to the existing literature on religious conversion, especially conversion from Christianity to Islam, in regard to the conversion process. My findings contribute to the existing literature that conversion to a new religion is a long, gradual process involving studying of literature, listening to preaching or teaching of the religion, observing lifestyle of other members, and comparing their religion of origin and the new religion of interest.

This study also contributes toward supporting previous research reasons identified to influence religious conversion. In addition, two motifs not discovered by Lofland and Skonovod's theory of conversion motifs were discovered. One of these two new motifs has more recently been discovered and is reported in the review on the literature I reported for this study. However, this is the first study, to my knowledge, to discover that an individual can change to a new religion because it would enable him become a minister and still get married, even when there are other denominations in his religion of origin that allow for this possibility as well. For example, one convert in this study was being trained to become a Reverend Father, but his late mother wanted him to have a family so she could have grandchildren. He converted to Islam where he could achieve this desire, as well as fulfill his late mother's wish. One would have expected him to join another denomination in Christianity that allows ministers to have a family instead of changing to Islam to fulfill this goal.

Furthermore, the findings identify for the first time, according to the literature examined, that most of the reasons that influenced the early Igbo converts to Islam are different from the reasons that influence contemporary Igbo converts to Islam.[22] Igbo early conversion to Islam was affectional according to Ottenberg's research while the current conversion is intellectual.

Considering Gerlach and Hine's seven stages of conversion and Rambo's model, my findings show that five stages of their models were applicable in contemporary Igbo conversions. Thus, my study contributes to scholarship by showing that stages of conversion could be seven or less, depending on the context of the research.

Last, although this study was conducted in different regions of Igboland, the findings suggest that this qualitative approach of discovering reported reasons why Christians convert to Islam would be beneficial in other parts of Africa. Repeating the research in other parts of Africa to compile more extensive data will allow social scientists to deepen their understanding of conversion, especially from Christianity to Islam, and especially in Africa. This in turn, will provide social scientists a better foundation to predict, and thus prepare, for future changes in the African social landscape.

The Church in Igboland

My findings can contribute considerably to the knowledge of the state of the church in Igboland. Though Igboland is known as the most populous Christian region, and most homogenous society, it is gradually being infiltrated by a foreign religion. Most of the churches in Igboland are ignorant of this trend, while those who are aware deem it inconsequential. My findings

---

22. Ottenberg, "Moslem Igbo Village," 240.

show that mainline churches in Igboland (especially Catholic and Anglican) are in a nominal state.

Missiology

This study reinforces the recommendation for the retention of contextualization in missiology. My findings show how Islam is being contextualized in Igboland; the converts become Muslims without losing their identity as Igbo. Some Christian institutions are discarding intercultural studies and thus undermining contextualization. My findings confirm the need for more research on religious conversion, especially from Christianity to Islam. Understanding this phenomenon can enable mission theorists to provide contemporary strategies to mitigate Islamic penetration into Christian regions. Also, it confirms the need for more laborers in the mission fields.

To the Researcher

The findings of my study opened my eyes to the reality of conversion to Islam in Igboland. I was completely ignorant of this phenomenon and its gradual, but steady, occurrence. This research has contributed to my knowledge of religious conversion, factors that influence religious conversion, reported reasons why Igbo Christians are converting to Islam, and the state of the church in Igboland, especially the impact of pastors charging dues payments to their members. I further understood that transformation can occur in any religion, in addition to Christianity. Interestingly, I now know and believe that Igbo people can actually become Muslims. The research has equally broadened my knowledge on various understandings of the conversion process that exists in Christian denominations as well.

Recommendations

To the Church in Igboland

The church in Igboland must be aware of this emerging trend in Igboland. Islam is penetrating Igboland through other Igbo Muslims, not Hausa. The church should wake up from her slumber, nominalism, prosperity gospel, and unnecessary financial dues imposed on its members. To accomplish this, the church needs to return to the teaching of the Bible, discipleship, and mentorship. She should eliminate and abolish the dues imposed on the members, especially as such dues are linked to the church's refusal to bury their (members) dead or give them succor in time of need, sickness, and lack, the opposite of the love and concern Christians are supposed to show to others.

Many people popularly claim that the Igbo who are converting to Islam do so for the financial and economic gains, so their conversion is not taken seriously. But this is a fallacy that keeps the church from taking this phenomenon seriously, because she erroneously assumes that those Igbo converts to Islam will return to Christianity after benefiting from Islam. This research shows that the majority of the converts were already educated, gainfully employed, had families, and were well settled in life prior to their conversion. Thus, their conversion was not influenced by these material gains, but rather primarily by the rationality of Islam, negative (hypocritical) lifestyle of Christians, financial demands from the church, as well as doctrinal liberalism and worldliness exhibited as follows.

Quest for church growth. In the face of several years of struggles to grow a church branch without success, pastors are usually under the temptation to whittle down pastoral disciplines. Restraints from carelessly throwing open the doors of the church to all comers, grow weaker and weaker by the day. Solutions on how to handle the wheat and the tares' in the church do exist but emphasis is usually given to bringing them in than attending to them. Inadequate hands to handle the classified church members is also a challenge. For instance, having men with the requisite spiritual experiences to handle the "crowd," the "young converts," the "growing believers" and those considered as "workers," is usually herculean. What would this breed? New and old wine mixed together in the same wine skin.

The challenge of the sinner-friendly approach. Again, it is not bad for a church to adopt to be sinner-friendly. After all, what does the church exist for if not to reach sinners and lead them to transformation? Was there any sinner that the Lord turned away? None! So, what's the problem? It is in approach. Before the Lord dived into the den of sinners, he had his strategies well worked out. There is no sinner the Lord Jesus ever talked to, befriended or visited that ultimately did not repent. Today, I am afraid the church is lacking in strategy. Different forms of programs are mounted to bring sinners the way they are into the church, but there is no deliberate discipleship effort to get these sinners transformed. Over a time, they get used to church language and mannerism but the manifestations that flow from within becomes a challenge.

The impact of the New World Order on the church. The New World Order is manifesting itself in dressing styles, music, dance, etc. The church, rather than firmly stand on its principles, struggles to adopt the New Age philosophy into church to attract the practitioners. But after bringing them in, the church stops there and in no distant time, compromise sets in. Soul winning is just a peripheral part of the job; discipleship is the main duty. But how many pastors spend time to disciple? Several pastors are even running away from pastoral jobs; they just want to do the work of the evangelist. The reporting system that premises pastoral success on number of souls in the church also brings pressure to bear on pastors to be less strict in discipline so that no church member drops on account of demands to put away certain ungodly attitudes or appearances.

Greed on the part of ministers of God. There are so many trending things in today's church. We hear of "our market day." A minister once confided in us (PFN Executive) that he does not play with his market day. He does not accept ministrations outside his church on Sundays because that's the day most church members come and that translates to bigger offering and tithes. This is true but such perception is wrongly placed. Sorry to say that in church today, several pastors are themselves products of such concepts and no wonder they see nothing wrong in the method. The quest to increase the wealth base of the church, has more than any other thing, introduced worldliness into the church. The pastor loses the authority to decide what happens in that church. Whether born or not born again, front seats belong to such men, excusing their sins feature regularly in the sermons, consultation with them on church policies become a must, etc. This is the same reason why church titles are on sale. The effect of worldliness in the church occasioned by greed of preachers is legion.

There is an urgent need for indigenization and acculturation of the gospel in Igboland; Igbo ways of life must replace Western ways of life. The gospel presented by the early missionaries came with Western baggage and modern-day preachers have continued in that pattern. For this change to occur, pastors need thorough biblical training, along with understanding its relevance in Igbo culture, beliefs, practices, and worldview. Pastors need to contextualize the gospel in a way that is appropriate for the Igbo people, so they can own the gospel. Both the gospel and Christianity need to be culturally integrated for it to have a deeply transformative and lasting impact in Igboland.

Second, Igbo Christians and pastors need to start living in accordance to the Bible and their preaching. They need to take seriously their profession as Christians and be serious with the things of God. Most of the converts attributed their turning to Islam to the negative lifestyle of some Christians, even pastors.

Third, Christians (both children and adults) need to know what they really believe and be well discipled. This can be accomplished by the church intentionally teaching members the doctrines of the Bible, leading them to trust in Jesus alone for eternal life, discipling through both discipleship programs and mentorship. The family equally needs to expose their children early to God, the Bible, and the church. Also, the Christians need to be taught and equipped specifically about Islam and how to counter Muslim claims and misunderstandings, such as the oneness of the Christian God (Trinity). As evident in this study, most of the converts to Islam seemed not to have accurate understanding of the salvation story and accurate understanding of the Bible stories, so they were unable to respond to Igbo Muslims' questions concerning the Bible.

To the Igbo Christian People

The Igbo people should make burial simple, stripped to its bear minimum, so that the poor can also bury their dead with dignity. There should be a standardized, acceptable, and affordable way of burying the dead to which the communities commit. For example, the dead must be buried within three to seven days, the bereaved are not required to throw a party or celebration to feed the crowd, rather sympathizers should come with food and money to support the bereaved.

To CAPRO Missionaries in Igboland and the Church

The missionaries serving in Igboland should read keenly chapter 4 of this dissertation to know and understand various reasons responsible for Igbo conversion to Islam. They need to provide tracts addressing each of the doctrinal and theological objections to the Bible, like the doctrine of the Trinity, Sonship of Jesus Christ, and prophethood of Mohammad.

To the Igbo Muslims in Igboland

The Igbo Muslims need to know and understand that Islam is gaining ground in Igboland through Igbo, not Hausa, as many Igbo are embracing Islam. Igbo Muslims need to build mosques in areas where there are many Igbo willing and ready to embrace Islam and worship, but unable to do so because of the lack of mosques. The Igbo Muslims, to preserve Igbo culture, must not engage in jihad (or killing of fellow Igbo) in the name of a religious war. They must not allow Hausa Muslims to detect how they practice Islam in Igboland and allow fundamental Islam to destroy Igbo culture.

Limitations of the Study and Recommendations for Future Research

The limitations of my study are addressed as implicit recommendations for future research. First and foremost, this study is limited in gender. Few female converts to Islam were involved in this study and most of them converted for marriage purposes, except one. This one convert was already married prior to conversion. This will enable us to discover whether interfaith marriage in Igboland is sole link to conversion to Islam for Igbo women. The findings of further investigations in this area will equally help us ascertain if conversion to Islam in Igboland occurs more among men than women. I had great difficulty accessing Igbo women converts to Islam, but there are good numbers of indigenous Muslim women.

Second, the data collection instruments adopted were insufficient to ascertain the depth of their claimed change of life or transformation. I adopted in-depth, face-to-face interviews and observation for my qualitative research method. I think further study is required, using participant observation, to discover if the converts' claimed change of life is really deep or superficial. Also, family members of these converts, pastors, and church members who knew them while they were Christians, should also be interviewed to confirm their claimed level of transformation and reported motivations for conversion.

Additionally, further research needs to be conducted on the perception and practice of jihad among Igbo Muslims. It is outside the scope of my study, but some reference appeared in the data collected. Further investigation is needed to ascertain if it involves killing of non- Igbo Muslims, as Hausa Muslims believe and practice.

Furthermore, research on the kind of relationship that exists between Igbo Muslims and Hausa Muslims is required. One convert in this study insinuated that Hausa Muslims hate the Igbo Muslims, while several others claimed that real Muslims overall are loving and caring. Is this care and love conditional?

Lastly, being up to date in dues payments demanded by the church before receiving assistance or burial was one of the contributing factors for conversion to Islam. Further investigation in needed to ascertain how other Igbo Christians respond to this issue.

Bibliography

Afigbo, E. "The Nsukka Communities from the Earlier Times to 1951: An Introductory Survey." *Okikpe* 3, no. 1 (1997): 1–26.

Amadi, L. E. *Igbo Heritage: Curriculum Materials for Social and Literary Studies.* Owerri: Imo Onyeukwu Press, 1987

Arinze, Francis A. *Sacrifice in Ibo Religion.* Ibadan: Ibadan University Press, 1970.

Austin-Broos, Diane. "The Anthropology of Conversion: An Introduction." In *The Anthropology of Religious Conversion*, edited by Andrew Buckser and Stephen D. Glazier, 1–12. Lanham, MD: Rowman & Littlefield, 2003.

Ayandele, Emmanuel A. "The Collapse of 'Pagandom' in Igboland." *Journal of the Historical Society of Nigeria* 7, no. 1 (December, 1973): 125–140.

Baer, Marc David. "History and Religious Conversion." In *The Oxford Handbook of Religious Conversion*, edited by Lewis R. Rambo and Charles E. Farhadian, 25–47. New York: Oxford University Press, 2014.

———. *Honored by the Glory of Islam: Conversion and Conquest in Ottoman Europe.* New York: Oxford University Press, 2011.

Barth, Christoph. "Notes on 'Return' in the Old Testament." *The Ecumenical Review* 19, no. 3 (July 1967): 310–312.

Battad, Do. "Sacrament of Baptism Is Necessary for Salvation." *Infallible Catholic* (blog), 24 February 2013. Accessed 6 February 2017. http://infallible-catholic.blogspot.com/2013/02/sacrament-of-baptism-is-necessary-for.html.

Bent, Ans van der. "The Concept of Conversion in the Ecumenical Movement: A Historical and Documentary Survey." *The Ecumenical Review* 44, no. 4 (October 1992): 380–390.

Bromiley, Geoffrey W., ed. *The International Standard Bible Encyclopedia.* Fully revised edition. Grand Rapids, MI: Eerdmans, 1988.

Brown, Colin, ed. *The New International Dictionary of New Testament Theology.* Volume 1. Exeter: Paternoster, 1975.

Bryant, M. Darrol and Christopher Lamb. *Religious Conversion : Contemporary Practices and Controversy.* London: Continuum International, 1999.

Buckser, Andrew, and Stephen D. Glazier. *The Anthropology of Religious Conversion.* Lanham, MD: Rowman & Littlefield, 2003.

Buxton, Sir Thomas Fowell. *The African Slave Trade, and Its Remedy*. London: J. Murray, 1840.

Cacioppo, John T. and Richard E. Petty. *Attitudes and Persuasion: Classic and Contemporary Approaches*. Boulder, CO: Westview Press, 1996.

Clarke, P. B. "The Methods and Ideology of the Holy Ghost Fathers in Eastern Nigeria 1885–1905." *Journal of Religion in Africa* 6, no. 2 (1974): 81–108.

Clines, David J. A., ed. *The Dictionary of Classical Hebrew*. Volume 8. Sheffield: Sheffield Academic Press, 2011.

Creswell, John W. *Educational Research: Planning, Conducting, and Evaluating Quantitative and Qualitative Research*. 4th ed. London: Harlow Pearson Education, 2014.

———. *Research Design: Qualitative and Quantitative Approaches*. Thousand Oaks, CA: SAGE, 1994.

———. *Research Design: Qualitative, Quantitative and Mixed Methods Approaches*. Thousand Oaks, CA: SAGE, 2003.

Dike, Ibrahim. "Igbo Conversion to Islam." Interview with Chinyere Priest, July 2015.

Dike, Victor E. "The Osu Caste System in Igbo Land: Discrimination Based on Descent." Paper presented at the Committee on the Elimination of Racial Discrimination Conference in Geneva, Switzerland, August 2002. Accessed 4 July 2014. http://www.nigerdeltapeoplesworldcongress.org/articles/osu_caste_system_in.pdf.

Dikki, Michael Ezra. "A Missiological Study of Islamic Strategies for Converting Christians to Islam and Their Implications for Christian Discipleship: A Study of Converts in Kawangware and Embul-Bul Areas of Nairobi-Kenya." Thesis, MDiv. Mission Studies, Africa International University, 2011.

Dimond, Brother Peter. *Outside the Catholic Church There Is Absolutely No Salvation*. 2nd ed. Filmore, NY: Most Holy Family Monastery, 2006.

Dodd, Charles Harold. *The Founder of Christianity*. London: Collins, 1971.

Doi, Abdur Rahman I. *Islam in Nigeria*. Zaria: Gaskiya Corp., 1984.

DomNwachukwu, Peter Nlemadim. *Authentic African Christianity: An Inculturation Model for the Igbo*. New York: P. Lang, 2000.

Dunne, Tad. "6. Authentic Feminist Doctrine." In *Lonergan and Feminism*, edited by Cynthia S. W. Crysdale, 114–133. Toronto: University of Toronto Press, 1994.

Dzurgba, Akpenpuun. *God and Caesar: A Study in the Sociology of Religion*. Ibadan: John Archers Publishers Limited, 2002.

Eaton, Richard M. "Approaches to the Study of Conversion to Islam in India." In *Approaches to Islam in Religious Studies*, edited by Richard C. Martin, 106–123. Tucson, AZ: University of Arizona Press, 1985.

Ekechi, F. K. "Colonialism and Christianity in West Africa: The Igbo Case, 1900–1915." *The Journal of African History* 12, no. 1 (January 1971): 103–115.

Ezeanya, Stephen N. "The Osu (Cult-Slave) System in Igbo Land." *Journal of Religion in Africa* (January 1967): 35–45.

Farhadian, Charles E. and Lewis R. Rambo. *The Oxford Handbook of Religious Conversion*. New York: Oxford University Press, 2014.

Fisher, Humphrey J. "Conversion Reconsidered: Some Historical Aspects of Religious Conversion in Black Africa." *Africa: Journal of the International African Institute* 43, no. 1 (January 1973): 27–40.

Geertz, Clifford. *The Religion of Java*. Glencoe, IL: The Free Press, 1960.

Gerlach, Luther P., and Virginia H. Hine. "Five Factors Crucial to the Growth and Spread of a Modern Religious Movement." *Journal for the Scientific Study of Religion* 7, no. 1 (1968): 23–40.

———. *People, Power, Change: Movements of Social Transformation*. Indianapolis: Bobbs-Merrill, 1970.

Gilliland, Dean S., and Charles H. Kraft, eds. *Appropriate Christianity*. Pasadena, CA: William Carey Library, 2005.

Glazier, Stephen D. "'Limin' wid Jah': Spiritual Baptists Who Become Restafarians and then Become Spiritual Baptists Again" In *The Anthropology of Religious Conversion*, edited by Andrew Buckser and Stephen D. Glazier, 149–170. Lanham, MD: Rowman & Littlefield, 2003.

Glesne, Corrine. *Becoming Qualitative Researchers: An Introduction*. Boston: Pearson Education, 2006.

Goetzmann, J. "Metanoia." In *The New International Dictionary of New Testament Theology*, edited by Colin Brown, volume 1, 357–359. Exeter: Paternoster Press, 1975.

Gooren, Henri. "Anthropology of Religious Conversion." In *The Oxford Handbook of Religious Conversion*, edited by Lewis R. Rambo and Charles E. Farhadian, 84–116. New York: Oxford University Press, 2014.

Greene, M. "The Lived World, Literature and Education." In *Phenomenology and Education Discourse*, edited by D. Vandenberg, 169–190. Johannesburg: Heinemann, 1997.

Hale, F. "Debating Igbo Conversion to Christianity: A Critical Indigenous View." *Acta Theologica* 26, no. 2 (2006): 116–135.

Hamilton, Victor P. s.v. "Shub." In *Theological Wordbook of the Old Testament*, edited by R. Laird Harris, Gleason L. Archer, and Bruce K. Waltke. Chicago: Moody Press, 1980.

Heirich, Max. "Change of Heart: A Test of Some Widely Held Theories About Religious Conversion." *American Journal of Sociology* 83, no. 3 (November 1977): 653–680.

Heikkinen, Jacob W. "'Conversion': A Biblical Study." National Faith and Order Colloquium, World Council of Churches, 12–17 June, 1966.

Horton, Robin. "African Conversion." *Africa: Journal of the International African Institute* 41, no. 2 (April 1971): 85–108.

Hudson, Deal W. "The Catholic View of Conversion." In *Handbook of Religious Conversion*, edited by H. Newton Malony and Samuel Southard, 108–122. Birmingham, AL: Religious Education Press, 1992.

Ifeka-Moller, Caroline. "White Power: Social-Structural Factors in Conversion to Christianity, Eastern Nigeria, 1921–1966." *Canadian Journal of African Studies* 8, no. 1 (January 1974): 55–72.

Igboin, Benson Ohihon. "Bias and Conversion: An Evaluation of Spiritual Transformation." *Evangelical Review of Theology* 37, no. 2 (April 2013): 166–182.

Ikenga-Metuh, Emefie. "The Shattered Microcosm: A Critical Survey of Explanations of Conversion in Africa." In *Religion, Development, and African Identity*, edited by Kirsten Holst Petersen, 11–27. Uppsala: Scandinavian Institute of African Studies, 1987.

Ilogu, Edmund Christopher Onyedum. *Christianity and Igbo Culture: A Study of the Interaction of Christianity and Igbo Culture*. New York: NOK, 1974.

Isichei, Elizabeth. *A History of the Igbo People*. London: Macmillan, 1976.

———. "Ibo and Christian Beliefs: Some Aspects of a Theological Encounter." *African Affairs* 68, no. 271 (April 1969): 121–134.

———. "Seven Varieties of Ambiguity: Some Patterns of Igbo Response to Christian Missions." *Journal of Religion in Africa* 3, no. 3 (January 1970): 209–227.

Jacob, Edmond. *Theology of the Old Testament*. New York: Harper & Row, 1958.

James, William, and Matthew Bradley. *The Varieties of Religious Experience*. Oxford: Oxford University Press, 2012.

Kalu, Ogbu. *The Embattled Gods: Christianization of Igboland, 1841–1991*. Lagos: Minaj, 1996.

Kerr, Hugh T., and John M. Mulder, eds. *Famous Conversions: The Christian Experience*. Grand Rapids, MI: Eerdmans, 1983.

Kim, Heon Choul and Ali Ulvi Mehmedoglu. "Conversion Motifs: A Study of Present-day South Korean Converts to Islam." *Journal of Academic Studies* 4, no. 15 (2003): 123–127.

Koehler, Ludwig, and Walter Baumgartner. *The Hebrew and Aramaic Lexicon of the Old Testament*. Volume 4. Leiden: Brill, 1999.

Koehler, Ludwig, Walter Baumgartner, M. E. J. Richardson, and Johann Jakob Stamm. *The Hebrew and Aramaic Lexicon of the Old Testament*. Study edition. Leiden; Boston: Brill, 2001.

Köse, Ali, and Kate Miriam Loewenthal. *Conversion to Islam: A Study of Native British Converts*. London: Routledge, 1996.

Kümmel, Werner Georg. *Man in the New Testament*. Philadelphia: Westminster Press, 1963.

Kunhiyop, Samuel Waje. *Christian Conversion in Africa: The Bajju Experience*. Jos: ECWA Productions, 2005.

Laubach, F. "Epistrepho." In *The New International Dictionary of New Testament Theology*, edited by Colin Brown, volume 1, 354–362. Exeter: Paternoster, 1975.

Lofland, John. *Doomsday Cult: A Study of Conversion, Proselytization, and Maintenance of Faith*. Englewood Cliffs, NJ: Prentice-Hall, 1966.

Lofland, John, and Norman Skonovd. "Conversion Motifs." *Journal for the Scientific Study of Religion* (1981): 373–385.

Lofland, John, and Rodney Stark. "Becoming a World-Saver: A Theory of Conversion to a Deviant Perspective." *American Sociological Review* 30, no. 6 (December 1965): 862–875.

Lonergan, Bernard J. F. *Method in Theology*. Toronto: University of Toronto Press, 1990.

Malony, H. N. "Conversion." In *The International Standard Bible Encyclopedia*, edited by Geoffrey W. Bromiley, volume 1, 768–770. Grand Rapids, MI: Eerdmans, 1988.

Manus, Chris Ukachukwu. "The Concept of Death and the After-Life in the Old Testament and Igbo Traditional Religion." *Mission Studies* 3, no. 1 (January 1986): 41–46.

Marshall, Catherine, and Gretchen B. Rossman. *Designing Qualitative Research*. 5th ed. Los Angeles: Sage, 2011.

Marshall-Fratani, Ruth. "Mediating the Global and Local in Nigerian Pentecostalism." *Journal of Religion in Africa* 28, no. 3 (August 1998): 278–315.

Mason, Jennifer. *Qualitative Researching*. London; Thousand Oaks, CA: Sage, 2002.

Mbah, Peter, and Eze C. Okonkwo. "Trade, Islam, and Politics in Northern Igboland: Ibagwa and Enugu Ezike Experience up to 1970." *Afro Asian Journal of Social Sciences* 2, no. 3.1 (2012): 1–15. Available online http://www.onlineresearchjournals.com/aajoss/art/81.pdf.

Mbiti, John S. *African Religions and Philosophy*. London: Heinemann, 1990.

McKinney, Carol Virginia. "The Bajju of Central Nigeria: A Case Study of Religious and Social Change." PhD diss., Southern Methodist University, 1985. Accessed 23 January 2017. https://www.sil.org/resources/archives/9788.

Mendoza, Marcela. "Converted Christians, Shamans, and the House of God: The Reasons for Conversion Given by the Western Toba of the Argentine Chaco." In *The Anthropology of Religious Conversion*, edited by Andrew Buckser and Stephen D. Glazier, 199–208. Lanham, MD: Rowman & Littlefield, 2003.

Merriam, Sharan B. *Qualitative Research: A Guide to Design and Implementation*. San Francisco, CA: John Wiley & Sons, 2009.

Meyer, Birgit. *Translating the Devil: Religion and Modernity Among the Ewe in Ghana*. Edinburgh: Edinburgh University Press, 1999.

Mohd Khambali, Khadijah. "Interfaith Marriage and Religious Conversion: A Case Study of Muslim Converts in Sabah, Malaysia." Paper presented at International Conference on Behavioral, Cognitive and Psychological Sciences (BCPS 2011). Accessed 13 July 2017. https://www.researchgate.net/publication/253239476.

Motte, Mary. "Conversion: A Missiological Perspective." *The Ecumenical Review* 44, no. 4 (October 1992): 453–457.

Mugenda, Abel G. and Olive M. Mugenda. *Research Methods: Quantitative and Qualitative Approaches*. Nairobi: African Centre for Technology Studies , 1999.

Murad, Khurram. *Da'wah among Non-Muslims in the West: Some Conceptual and Methodological Aspects*. Leicester: The Islamic Foundation, 1986.

Nieuwkerk, Karin van. "'Islam Is Your Birthright'. Conversion, Reversion and Alternation. The Case of New Muslimas in the West." In *Cultures of Conversion*, edited by Jan N. Bremmer, Wout J. van Bekkum, and Arie L. Molendijk, 151–165. Leuven: Peeters, 2006.

Nnadozie, Emmanuel. "African Indigenous Entrepreneurship Determinants of Resurgence and Growth of Igbo Entrepreneurship During the Post-Biafra Period." *Journal of African Business* 3, no. 1 (January 2002): 49–80.

Nnorom, C. Aham. "Islam in Igboland: Lesson in History." Paper presented at the International Conference on Igbo Studies: A Tribute to Simon Ottenberg, Cornell University, New York, April 2003.

Nock, Arthur Darby. *Conversion: The Old and the New in Religion from Alexander the Great to Augustine of Hippo*. Baltimore, MD: John Hopkins University Press, 1998.

Norris Sachs, Rebecca. "Converting to What? Embodied Culture and the Adoption of New Beliefs." In *The Anthropology of Religious Conversion*, edited by Andrew Buckser and Stephen D. Glazier, 171–181. Lanham, MD: Rowman & Littlefield, 2003.

Nwagbara, Eucharia Nwabugo. "The Igbo of Southeast Nigeria: The Same Yesterday, Today and Tomorrow?" *Dialectical Anthropology* 31, nos. 1–3 (2007): 99–110.

Nwaka, Jacinta Chiamaka. "The Early Missionary Groups and the Contest for Igboland: A Reappraisal of Their Evangelization Strategies." *Missiology* 40, no. 4 (2012): 409–423.

Nwala, T. Uzodinma. *Igbo Philosophy*. Ikeja: Lantern Books, 1985.

Ojukwu, Chukwuemeka Odumegwu. *The Ahiara Declaration: The Principles of the Biafran Revolution*. Enugu: Biafra Information Service Corporation, 1969.

Okodo, Ikechukwu. "Igbo Man's Belief in Prayer for the Betterment of Life." *Journal of Religion and Human Relations* 1, no. 1 (2008).

Okorocha, Cyril C. *The Meaning of Religious Conversion in Africa: The Case of the Igbo of Nigeria*. Aldershot: Avebury, 1987.

Okwu, Augustine S. O. "The Weak Foundations of Missionary Evangelization in Precolonial Africa: The Case of the Igbo of Southeastern Nigeria 1857–1900." *Missiology* 8, no. 1 (1980): 31–49.

Orji, Cyril. *Ethnic and Religious Conflicts in Sub-Saharan Africa*. Milwaukee, WI: Marquette University Press, 2008.

Orji, Matthew O. *The History and Culture of the Igbo People before the Advent of the White Man*. Nkpor: Jet Publishers, 1999.

Ottenberg, Simon. "A Moslem Igbo Village." *Cahiers d'Études Africaines* 11 (1971): 231–260.

———. "Ibo Receptivity to Change." *Continuity and Change in African Cultures* (1959): 130–143.

———. "Thoughts on Islam in Southeastern Nigeria." In *New Face of Islam in Eastern Nigeria and the Lake Chad Basin: Essays in Honour of Simon Ottenberg*, edited by Egodi Uchendu, 1–37. Makurdi: Aboki Publishers, 2012.

Ozigboh, Ikenga R. A. *A History of Igboland in the 20th Century*. Enugu: Snaap Press, 1999.

Paloutzian, Raymond F. "Psychology of Religious Conversion and Spiritual Transformation." In *The Oxford Handbook of Religious Conversion*, edited by Lewis R. Rambo and Charles E. Farhadian, 209–239. New York: Oxford University Press, 2014.

Paloutzian, Raymond F., James T. Richardson, and Lewis R. Rambo. "Religious Conversion and Personality Change." *Journal of personality* 67, no. 6 (December 1999): 1047–1079.

Parameswaran, Ashvin and Rodney Sebastian. "Conversion and the Family: Chinese Hare Krishnas." *Journal of Contemporary Religion* 22, no. 3 (2007): 341–359.

Peace, Richard V. "Conflicting Understandings of Christian Conversion: A Missiological Challenge." *International Bulletin of Missionary Research* 28, no. 1 (2004): 8–14.

———. *Conversion in the New Testament: Paul and the Twelve*. Grand Rapids, MI: Eerdmans, 1999.

Pope Paul VI. "Evangelii Nuntiandi." 8 December 1975. Accessed 6 February 2017. http://w2.vatican.va/content/paul-vi/en/apost_exhortations/documents/hf_p-vi_exh_19751208_evangelii-nuntiandi.html.

Racius, Egdunas. "The Multiple Nature of the Islamic Da'Wa." PhD diss., University of Helsinki, 2004. http://ethesis.helsinki.fi/julkaisut/hum/aasia/vk/racius/themulti.pdf

Rambo, Lewis R. "Conversion: Toward a Holistic Model of Religious Change." *Pastoral Psychology* 38, no. 1 (1989): 47–63.

———. "Theories of Conversion: Understanding and Interpreting Religious Change." *Social Compass* 46, no. 3 (1999): 259–272.

———. "The Psychology of Conversion." In *Handbook of Religious Conversion*, edited by H. Newton Malony and Samuel Southard, 159–177. Birmingham, AL: Religious Education Press, 1992.

———. *Understanding Religious Conversion*. New Haven, CT: Yale University Press, 1993.

Reidhead, Mary Ann, and Van A. Reidhead. "From Jehovah's Witness to Benedictine Nun: The Roles of Experience and Context in a Double Conversion." In *The Anthropology of Religious Conversion*, edited by Andrew Buckser and Stephen D. Glazier, 183–197. Lanham, MD: Rowman & Littlefield, 2003.

Rink, Tobias. "An Interdisciplinary Perspective on Conversion." *Missionalia* 35, no. 2 (August 2007): 18–43.

Rossman, Gretchen B., and Sharon F. Rallis. *Learning in the Field: An Introduction to Qualitative Research*. Thousand Oaks, CA: Sage, 2012.

Rubin, Herbert J., and Irene S. Rubin. *Qualitative Interviewing: The Art of Hearing Data*. London: Sage, 2011.

Rufai, Saheed Ahmad. "A Foreign Faith in a Christian Domain: The Historical Development of Islam among the Igbos of Southeastern Nigeria." *Jurnal Hadhari* 4, no. 2 (2012): 137–154.

Sanneh, Lamin. *Translating the Message: The Missionary Impact on Culture*. New York: Orbis Books, 2015.

Schneirla, William S. "Conversion in the Orthodox Church." *St Vladimir's Seminary Quarterly* 11, no. 2 (1967): 87–95.

Seidman, Irving. *Interviewing as Qualitative Research: A Guide for Researchers in Education and the Social Sciences*. New York: Teachers College Press, 2013.

Spradley, James Phillip. *Participant Observations*. London; New York: Holt, Rinehart and Winston, 1980.

Starbuck, Edwin Diller. *Psychology of Religion: An Empirical Study of the Growth of Religious Consciousness*. London: Walter Scott, 1899.

Süss, Joachim, and Renate Pitzer-Reyl. *Religionswechsel: Hintergründe Spiritueller Neuorientierung*. München: Claudius Verlag, 1996.

Triulzi, Alessandro. "Trade, Islam, and the Mahdia in Northwestern Wallaggā, Ethiopia." *Journal of African History* 16, no. 1 (1975): 55–71.

Tynan, Mark. "New Evangelization, Conversion and Catholic Education." MPhil diss., University of Notre Dame (2013). Accessed 2 February 2017. http://researchonline.nd.edu.au/theses/97

Ubah, C. N. "Religious Change among the Igbo during the Colonial Period." *Journal of Religion in Africa* (1988): 71–91.

Uchendu, Egodi. *Dawn for Islam in Eastern Nigeria: A History of the Arrival of Islam in Igboland*. Berlin: K. Schwarz, 2011.

———. "Evidence for Islam in Southeast Nigeria." *The Social Science Journal* 47, no. 1 (2010): 172–188.

Uchendu, Victor Chikezie. *The Igbo of Southeast Nigeria*. New York: Holt, Rinehart & Winston, 1965.
Wallace, Anthony F. C. "Revitalization Movements." *American Anthropologist* 58, no. 2 (1956): 264–281.
Wallis, Jim. *The Call to Conversion: Recovering the Gospel for These Times*. New York: Harper & Row, 1981.
Walls, Andrew F. "Converts or Proselytes? The Crisis over Conversion in the Early Church." *International Bulletin of Missionary Research* 28, no. 1 (2004): 2–7.
Ware, Kallistos. *The Orthodox Way*. Crestwood, NY: St. Vladimir's Press, 1995.
Wikipedia. "Boko Haram." Last modified 21 October 2019 at 15.07 (UTC), https://en.wikipedia.org/wiki/Boko_Haram.
Wohlrab-Sahr, Monika. "Conversion to Islam: Between Syncretism and Symbolic Battle." *Social Compass* 46, no. 3 (1999): 351–362.
Woodberry, J. Dudley. "Conversion in Islam." In *Handbook of Religious Conversion*, edited by H. Newton Malony and Samuel Southard, 22–40. Birmingham, AL: Religious Education Press, 1992.
Yang, Fenggang, and Andrew Abel "Sociology of Religious Conversion." In *The Oxford Handbook of Religious Conversion*, edited by Lewis R. Rambo and Charles E. Farhadian, 140–163. New York: Oxford University Press, 2014.

Langham Literature, with its publishing work, is a ministry of Langham Partnership.

Langham Partnership is a global fellowship working in pursuit of the vision God entrusted to its founder John Stott –

> *to facilitate the growth of the church in maturity and Christ-likeness through raising the standards of biblical preaching and teaching.*

Our vision is to see churches in the Majority World equipped for mission and growing to maturity in Christ through the ministry of pastors and leaders who believe, teach and live by the word of God.

Our mission is to strengthen the ministry of the word of God through:
- nurturing national movements for biblical preaching
- fostering the creation and distribution of evangelical literature
- enhancing evangelical theological education

especially in countries where churches are under-resourced.

Our ministry

Langham Preaching partners with national leaders to nurture indigenous biblical preaching movements for pastors and lay preachers all around the world. With the support of a team of trainers from many countries, a multi-level programme of seminars provides practical training, and is followed by a programme for training local facilitators. Local preachers' groups and national and regional networks ensure continuity and ongoing development, seeking to build vigorous movements committed to Bible exposition.

Langham Literature provides Majority World preachers, scholars and seminary libraries with evangelical books and electronic resources through publishing and distribution, grants and discounts. The programme also fosters the creation of indigenous evangelical books in many languages, through writer's grants, strengthening local evangelical publishing houses, and investment in major regional literature projects, such as one volume Bible commentaries like the *Africa Bible Commentary* and the *South Asia Bible Commentary*.

Langham Scholars provides financial support for evangelical doctoral students from the Majority World so that, when they return home, they may train pastors and other Christian leaders with sound, biblical and theological teaching. This programme equips those who equip others. Langham Scholars also works in partnership with Majority World seminaries in strengthening evangelical theological education. A growing number of Langham Scholars study in high quality doctoral programmes in the Majority World itself. As well as teaching the next generation of pastors, graduated Langham Scholars exercise significant influence through their writing and leadership.

To learn more about Langham Partnership and the work we do visit **langham.org**

www.ingramcontent.com/pod-product-compliance
Lightning Source LLC
Chambersburg PA
CBHW070806230426
43665CB00017B/2503